# THIS GAMING LIFE

DIGITALCULTUREBOOKS
is a collaborative imprint of the
University of Michigan Press and the
University of Michigan Library.

# THIS GAMING LIFE

## TRAVELS IN THREE CITIES

Jim Rossignol

The University of Michigan Press AND The University of Michigan Library ▶ Ann Arbor

2011   2010   2009   2008      4   3   2   1

A CIP catalog record for this book is available from the British Library.

Library of Congress Cataloging-in-Publication Data

Rossignol, Jim, 1978–
     This gaming life : travels in three cities / Jim Rossignol.
          p.      cm.
     ISBN-13: 978-0-472-11635-5 (cloth : alk. paper)
     ISBN-10: 0-472-11635-5 (cloth : alk. paper)
     1. Video games—Social aspects.   2. Video games—Psychological
aspects.   I. Title.

     GV1469.34.S52R67    2008
     794.8–dc22                                              2007052485

Nobody leads a life of quiet desperation nowadays. The mass of men was quietly desperate a million years ago because the infernal computers inside their skulls were incapable of restraint or idleness; were forever demanding more challenging problems which life could not provide.

▶ KURT VONNEGUT, *Galápagos*, 1985

My friend Trevor is over at my house with his nephew Donny. We're playing *WarioWare* on the GameCube, but Donny's not really interested. When it came time to make a man jump on a banana, he pronounced it "gay" and put the controller down. So now it's down to me as a dancing cat and Trevor as some kind of alien in sunglasses and a cape. Donny's reading the manual for *Manhunt*. He's pretty psyched that you can kill someone with a plastic bag.

▶ TOM CHICK, "Saving Private Donny," 2004

# Contents

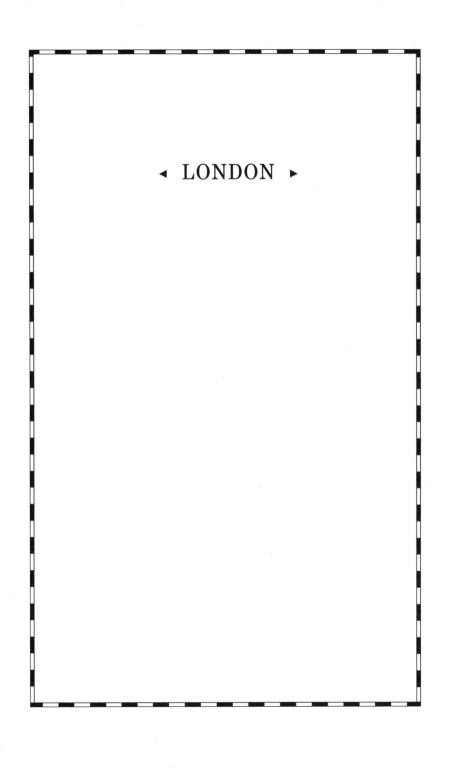

# ◄ LONDON ►

# How Games Make Gamers

## A NEW LIMB

In May 2000 I was fired from my job as a reporter on a finance newsletter because of an obsession with a video game. It was the best thing that ever happened to me.

The job had two parts. The first part was desperately dull but easy enough for me to bumble through. Each morning I drove out to a farmhouse office complex located deep in the English countryside and sat on a Herman Miller chair in front of a large curvilinear desk. There I processed articles about how to format corporate curricula vitae or occasionally attempted to make sense of the information I had gathered in the second part of my job. Most of the time, however, I spent clicking through a series of online forums where people discussed the ups and downs of recently released video games. Anything would do.

The second part of the job took place in London. Rising at dawn, I traveled up to Charing Cross in the old slam-door train carriages and watched in silent despair as the City drew ever closer. The country office might have been unapologetically quiet and slow, but the City was numbingly, achingly boring. I longed for someone to talk to, someone who was even remotely inclined to escape the world of banking. Inevitably I would find myself isolated in a seminar that focused on the workings of debit systems and direct payment pipelines. I would stand up, say my name and that of my employer, and then attempt to avoid speaking for the next four or five hours. I carefully filled my notepads with poorly understood jottings. As a graduate, I had assumed that I wanted to be a journalist of some kind, but I clearly wasn't coping with this. What should have been tight, insightful reporting ended up being vague, impressionistic, often unusable information. The world of finance remained a forbidding mystery, and the stack of John Kenneth Galbraith books by my bedside wasn't doing much to kindle my enthusiasm for economics either.

But there was something else going on in my life that ran parallel—almost contrary—to my suit-and-tie day job: a kind of double life. During my spare moments, I was submerged in a different activity, one in which I was completely at home. It was a video game called *Quake III Arena*. Gaming was a daily release, a few hours of energy and color to counterbalance my career in corporate tedium. With a cup of tea and late-1990s soundtrack (Britpop with a smattering of electronica), I launched myself into evenings of gleeful acrobatics. A torrent of explosions and power-ups vigorously erased the memories of boredom.

The *Quake* games are the direct descendants of that most notorious of modern video games, *Doom*. They are combat games set in a first-person perspective and filled with the latest in spectacular graphic effects. You control your character directly, seeing things from his or her perspective, shooting when you hit the trigger button, and picking up weapons and ammunition as you move. These games seem straightforward and approachable, since they are so close to how we experience things in real life—you run around, see things from the character's point of view, and so on. Yet the experience of *Quake* and its kin can be baffling for anyone who hasn't already sunk hours into mastering them. Beginners find themselves in a state of confusion, unable to avoid looking at the floor or the ceiling for extended periods. Bumping into walls, unable to aim, or finding yourself obliterated by your enemies—the list of frustrations grows by the second. And they are all due to a dastardly control system that expects you to maneuver a keyboard and mouse in unison (or two thumbsticks when playing on a gamepad)—no small feat for any novice. Then there's all the arcane rites involved in using a desktop PC to play games: install the patches, update the drivers, tweak the gizmometer. . . . This kind of gaming doesn't make itself easy, and it's tough to get yourself up to speed. Of course, anyone could, theoretically, pick up and play these games; yet, like riding a bike or driving a car, they'll need a guiding hand to get out on the road. At weekends and during spare evenings, I was such a guiding hand.

*Quake III* has the capacity to connect to "hosted" games on the Internet. This means that a dozen or so people can connect to a server and fight each other remotely from the comfort of attics, offices, and bedrooms across the world. They can make up ad hoc teams or simply run amok, blasting each other with rocket launchers and lightning guns. I played on these online servers for countless hours, chatting away, fighting, learning new techniques. In fact, the days and weeks I poured into playing this single game meant that I had become unnervingly precise. I soon played at a level that combined detailed knowledge of the game's workings with acute learned reflexes. To those who had just started playing, this kind of play seemed almost superhuman. The experienced few used weapon physics to fly up walls or demonstrated innate spatial awareness that defied tactical expectations of less experienced players. Landing a missile right on top of an enemy without having seen him for several minutes, just because you *knew* he would be right there, right then, became a routine experience. It was considered a great honor to be accused of cheating. How else indeed could anyone play a game with this kind of proficiency?

Being accused of cheating wasn't enough for me though, and I began to desire some kind of greater recognition for my dedication. I realized I could get something more out of the time I had invested: I could start my own team. Toward the end of the 1990s, games like *Quake* had become popular as competitive enterprises. Amateur teams played (and still play) scheduled matches over the Internet. Online leagues blossomed, and net-based communities were formed to help run the events. These communities provided servers for the online games and orchestrated league structures for the players to battle it out. I had already been involved in one casual online team while playing the *Quake* clone *Kingpin*, which had a theme of 1920s gang violence. So when *Quake III* was released in 1999, I decided to enter these new gladiatorial arenas with my own squad.

My initial recruitment plan consisted of simply talking to other players. Many of them had only ever played a few video games in their lifetime, having found the predictability and solitary focus of single-player games off-putting. But they experienced the online game as a revelation. Here was something more akin to a sport, with real spectators yelling hints from the sidelines and an army of human-controlled talent to show you how it was done. This human element transformed gaming for my players, and they each experienced minor epiphanies as they joined up with other, distant gamers for five-a-side *Quake* games of "capture the flag." "It was like exercising a new limb," recalled one gamer I spoke to about that time. "I was suddenly practicing and arranging matches every other night, as if I was in a pub footie team—even though no football team would ever have me!"

I knew how he felt. Cold mornings, adolescent disinterest, and a nagging hip injury had meant that I was banished from the sports field for many years. I wasn't going to be able to indulge in the camaraderie that sports teams felt or in the extended buzz of victory through dedication and cooperation. That entire swathe of experience had been cut off from me by cruel circumstance and a good dose of self-defeating apathy. Now, however, there was a possibility for some kind of redemption: a sport for the quick-fingered and the computer-bound; a space of possibility in which I could mold friends and strangers into a proficient gaming team.

And so I ran trials of sorts and trained players in how best to use *Quake III*'s many weapons. The first few signups came from one-on-one duels, which, by their nature, meant you usually got talking with the other person. Usually the conversations were with someone whose native language was Russian or Portuguese, so the experience was often bizarre, occasionally awkward, but sometimes fruitful and friendly. After a few good fights and swapped instant messenger names, the founding team members began to appear. My extensive reading of *Quake* forums and fan Web sites (combined with seemingly endless practice) meant that I could rapidly improve the averages of my new players. I showed them how setting the mouse pointer to a slower speed improved their accuracy and how the in-game graphics could be stripped down and reduced to create a smoother, clearer experience. It was like fine-tuning a car, only I had figured out how it all worked through Web sites, forum posts, and some reverse engineering of game files.

Meanwhile, things in the world of financial journalism lurched along in an uneven fashion. My poor performance had been noted, and I knew that the situation was a downward spiral. I dreaded the 6 a.m. starts that would land me in central London, and I longed to get back to my increasingly successful foray into team gaming. The discussions about corporate finance inexorably turned into indecipherable droning as my brain reduced the non-*Quake* signal to static. I plodded on, trying not to draw attention to the idle creaking of my expensive chair. I did what I could but began to receive fewer and fewer assignments. I was worried. I felt doomed.

The team, meanwhile, had just signed its essential star player. A natural talent and an astute tactician, he gave the team a vital edge. Almost a year after signing him, I met this prodigy at a games weekend in a small town in Devon. Paul was accompanied by his brother-in-law. He was an unassuming IT technician with a receding hairline. He had an expensive car and . . . , well, there's no accounting for people's taste in pop music. I think it's fair to say that we didn't really connect, but that didn't ultimately matter. Our shared interest in competitive *Quake* was all that we needed to worry about. The team needed Paul, and for at least a short time, Paul needed the team, too.

During that time, we entered competitions and even won a few prizes for participating in the demonstration matches that were shown on the early Internet TV station Network of the World. We knew that we could never beat the best that Europe had to offer, but our game nevertheless rose to the point where we began to hold our own against the lower echelons of the top few thousand *Quake* players. Even our casual play was now far from casual: we examined everything, analyzed every move in hour-long discussions after the games. I was by now an utterly obsessed player-coach. I arranged practice schedules and sparring teams to meet us on private servers. I watched recordings of famous matches, especially those featuring teams we were about to face. I filtered everything back to my players: game configurations that might give us an advantage, tactics that would give us the edge, player formations that might give my team members a split-second drop on their opponents. What my team lacked in raw skill with a rocket launcher they would make up for in preparation, computing finesse, and insider knowledge. I was delighted when I managed to snare top-class players and distraught when we weren't deemed talented enough to be worth their time. I constantly nursed egos in private chat rooms, trying to field the best team while at the same time giving everyone a go. "Honestly, Crazy Joe, you're a fine player, but the others turned up for more practice sessions . . ."

I cracked down on unsporting smack talk, gave (supposedly) rousing speeches (sometimes typed, then later over Internet voice communications), and played occasional Cupid between the extremely shy woman who had joined the team and the extremely shy man whom she clearly intended to hit on. We struggled, we played, we won, and we lost. We clawed our way up through the divisions. Each victory was a euphoric celebration, each loss a crippling disaster.

On the train to London, meanwhile, I routinely passed a placard advertising some kind of telephone help line. It asked me, in bright yellow-on-pink letters, "Are you cracking up?" I looked down at the frayed edges of my notebook and wondered how long all this could go on. How long could I hold down a job when my mind was lost in gaming? Was I lying to myself about even trying to be a journalist?

Soon thereafter the crucial moment came to pass. My manager, Richard, sat me down and fixed me with a clouded look. He had, he assumed, some bad news: "We're going to have to let you go."

The hallelujah chorus sounded. I felt the rush of sudden freedom: now there was nothing between me and pure indulgence. I could concentrate on the team seven days a week, without interruption, without tortuous journeys into the heart of finance. It was a moment of thrilling emancipation. I plunged into it, headfirst, playing for long days and late nights. Dawn was a familiar sight at bedtime. The team grew and became more cohesive. We found like-minded teams to spar with, allowing my players to grow more confident. Soon they could play *and* win.

Needless to say, my attempts to secure new employment were infrequent. Stacks of unprocessed job advertisements grew on either side of my desk, and my savings dwindled. Games refused to pay the bills, and I would eventually have to make a genuine effort to look for full-time employment. I made a few sullen forays to industrial parks and office blocks, and I even began to learn simple programming languages, but unbeknownst to me at the time, my break had already arrived. I had, thanks to the insistence of some friends, applied for a position on a games magazine. I expected nothing, didn't care, and told the interviewers much of the story you've been reading here. They conferred, unsure. Unsurprisingly I didn't get the job. But I did later receive a call asking whether I could possibly write something that would help the magazine's readers play a little better. I said I probably could and wondered if they could help me avoid having to return to London and the worrying question on the pink and yellow billboard. The answer was yes.

## BLEEPING AND ZAPPING

Video games changed my life. It's a pleasing convenience to be able to pinpoint a moment, or at least a period of time, that enables me to chart the change so precisely. Thanks to my *Quake* expertise, I was soon in a full-time job that didn't have anything to do with corporate treasury issues or early morning meetings in bank seminar rooms. It was a radical shift both professionally and personally, and it was almost entirely unexpected. After all, games might have been crucial to my day-to-day identity, but I had never admitted as much to myself. They were a distraction, an excellent waste of time. They had no specific value, and I never expected my obsession to pay the rent and focus my entire career.

As a games journalist, I went on to meet plenty of other people whose lives have been changed, defined—perhaps even saved—by gaming. Many of the gamers I've met have been involved directly in the games industry, but others are simply people for whom gaming is a continuous presence in their lives. Games have catalyzed major changes for some of these people, as they did for me. But they usually change us in subtler ways. These subtler effects have only begun to be mapped by researchers, commentators, and gamers. Sometimes the effects seem to be negative: people so distracted that they lose sight of their responsibilities—ignoring jobs, families, and everyday lives. Other times they are positive—stimulating intellectual and personal growth or awakening unrealized ambitions in creative minds. Gaming seems to be neither wholly positive nor entirely negative: its value (or lack thereof) is indistinct and undefined. Perhaps more critically still, many people lack the conceptual vocabulary to describe games in a positive way at all. One of the most routine complaints in the games industry is "My parents/partner/peers still don't believe I have a proper job." It's not just that many people don't take gaming seriously, they don't know how to take it seriously. And why would they, if their only experience of it was a drunken game of *NHL Hockey* after a night out at a singles bar or the weird Japanese cartoon creatures that a younger brother or sister seems to care so much about?

I am going to try to persuade you here that games are worth paying attention to. They are worth taking seriously and thinking and talking about in some detail. They might even be a very good thing for our culture as a whole. But what is most important to my analysis is the fact of video games' ambiguous social value: they're beloved by gamers and derided or dismissed by the uninitiated. Of course, I might not be able to resolve that ambiguity, but I do intend to offer snapshots of gaming life that will make it a little clearer why gamers themselves value games—or at least some games—to the extent they do.

My generation is the first to live their entire lives in the company of electronic, interactive entertainment. We see the TV as a facilitator of rhythm-action rapping games as much as a way to tune into the daily news. Our expectations of what a game should be are defined not by sports, chess, or a deck of cards but by gamepads, plasma screens, and motion sensors. Our cultural backdrop is defined by exposure to a constantly evolving repertoire of technologies, technology that seems to stake out new territory for itself with each passing month: we do not expect things to stay the same. We expect newness and change. Video games represent some of the most sophisticated computing and programming technologies available: a supercomputer in every home and a complex networking gaming platform on every mobile phone. It's a technology that we expect to evolve. Games get prettier, faster, louder, and more expensive. Yet today's consumers experience this rapid evolution of electronic gaming as just another element of everyday life, as commonplace as TV shows, Italian food, or shopping.

Nevertheless, many of the gamers I encounter report the same experience of feeling as if they have engaged in some kind of transgression. There's often a sense of guilt that comes with tales of gaming exploits, as if games were a vice or a character flaw, a symptom of one kind or another. I began to take note of these reports and often found myself wondering what it was that people were really doing when they were playing video games: was it an obsession with pretty colors or with sheer novelty? Was it something deeper? Were people getting anything worthwhile out of games at all? Some researchers have begun to examine this question in some detail. Work carried out by psychologist Richard Wood and his colleagues at Nottingham Trent University included an online questionnaire in which gamers answered questions about their habits. A majority reported that they felt as if they were "wasting time" playing games, and yet most of them were hard pressed to identify what else they should have been doing with that time. Reading a book, perhaps? That was one popular answer.

I asked Henry Jenkins, the smiling, bearded codirector of the MIT Comparative Media Studies program, why he thought so many gamers gave this kind of response. Jenkins observed that many activities can be engaged with productively or unproductively and that games were no exception—a lot of the gamers probably *were* wasting their time by playing games. Yet there was another force at work here, one that he was keen to identify: "Most of us are overscheduled and overburdened with other aspects of our lives, and it ought to be a sacred thing to sometimes goof off with our mates," said Jenkins. "But I think the issue goes deeper than that. We lack ways of justifying or explaining the value of games as a meaningful form of activity. They are under fire from all sides. Most people treat them as debased and unproductive. And we start to feel guilty because we internalize some of those perceptions and descriptions."

I believe that the nature of those "perceptions and descriptions" is an important part of identifying what it means to be a gamer and how that identity could—and perhaps should—change. Games, particularly in the West, have been identified with a nerdy subculture and still carry negative social connotations. In some cases, games are actively vilified. The British parliamentarian Boris Johnson described the effects of video games like this: "The nippers [children] are bleeping and zapping in speechless rapture, their passive faces washed in explosions and gore. They sit for so long that their souls seem to have been sucked down the cathode-ray tube. They become like blinking lizards, motionless, absorbed, only the twitching of their hands showing they are still conscious. These machines teach them nothing. They stimulate no ratiocination, discovery, or feat of memory."

Jon Henshaw, the editor of parenting Web site Family Resource.com, offers a similar, if somewhat less sensational, description of what gamers are doing: "Instead of taking a trip, mountain biking, or hanging out with friends at a café, gamers spend their time in a virtual reality. Whereas real-life experiences bear long-lasting friendships and memories, video games do not. The only pictures that come from video games are screenshots, and the memories that are created from playing those games are ultimately meaningless."

Could the experience of gaming really be "meaningless"? It's a given that many games (like many books or films) are badly made and trashy, but are the souls of gamers actually suffering under the glare of this digital menace? My own life was changed for the better thanks to the expertise I gleaned through habitual gaming, but it seems clear to me that there's something else to be earned from the act itself, something positive about simply spending a few hours a week playing games. The gamers I meet aren't vacant-eyed zombies or "blinking lizards." They (usually) have smiles on their faces, and they express lively opinions on what they've seen on many different types of gaming screens. So my cards are on the table: I'm going to offer some alternative, positive descriptions. This analysis will show how video games have inspired artists, transformed rags into riches, given purpose to empty lives, and entertained bored people on a Sunday afternoon. We'll see how games turned young people into heroes and how gaming has enabled the realization of previously unimaginable ambitions. We'll see how games can make us better people, how they dissolve the horrors of boredom—and how they can function as propaganda for a wide range of worthy and unworthy causes.

## MONSTER RETURNING

Despite a deluge of positive images of hip, popular gamers since Disney's *Tron* in 1982, games in the media have long been dogged by negative descriptions. Games are routinely associated with "youth in crisis," and stories about obesity or falling educational scores are often illustrated by stock footage of gamers at play. Like other forms of new media before them (pulp fiction, comics, rock and roll, film, TV), games have been portrayed as harmful, morally and socially. And they seem to be particularly hazardous to the mental and physical health of the young. Yet in years of reporting on games, I've uncovered little evidence for such claims; nor is this supposed degradation evident in my own life or in the lives of the people around me. (Was I really fired because of an obsession with a game, or was I simply in the wrong job?)

I'm going to supply some unambiguously positive descriptions of gaming and of gamers that I hope will, among other things, enable gamers to identify the value in their pastime and, ultimately, find even more productive and meaningful ways of engaging with it. Most of the time, of course, we will be simply "goofing off" playing *Grand Theft Auto,* but perhaps gamers and others will eventually be able to see that, too, as sacred.

One gamer for whom fresh descriptions of gaming are nothing new is the experimental installation artist Brody Condon. He creates artworks that are influenced as much by his video game experiences as by the emotional and social traumas that he feels define him as a human being. His work offers strange visions of gamelike figures: a computerized Elvis toting an AK-47, a thousand consecutive deaths of video game characters, a battle of performance art in an LA gallery, a sculpture of a famous game developer as he appears inside his own game.

Like many other gamers, Condon feels that much of his own personality has been shaped by gaming: "I was born the same year *SpaceWar* was created. I was the juvenile delinquent at the local arcades before they disappeared. I took over [role-playing sessions] if our usual Saturday afternoon scenario creator, a Presbyterian minister and religious school vice principal who still lived with his mother, was sick. I subscribed to *Nintendo Power Magazine.* Floppy disks came in the mail. I dressed up in fantasy armor and beat my friends over the head with sticks and foam. I sat in a closet in front of a hand-me-down TI-99 and programmed text-based adventure games that I would lose as soon as I turned the damn thing off. I was 'the kid that could beat any game' at my shitty public school."

These experiences provided Condon with his unique visual language when he eventually studied art. Games gave him a way of working that was all his own and, in doing so, enabled the artist to create himself. "These days, whenever I meet actual game developers or speak at game conferences, I feel like a kind of Frankenstein," explained Condon as he talked to me about the connection between games and his art. "I've been playing their games my whole life, you know? And here I am, like the monster returning to the master that created it, arms outstretched, mumbling, 'Give my life meaning.'"

Condon, like most artists, takes his cues from the world he is presented with, and much of that world consists of video games. If games have value here, it's in providing Condon with a focus and language for his work and the inspiration to create it. What Condon does is recognized as art in the gallery sense, with its visually striking juxtapositions and video game materials presented out of context. In fact, game-related video installations and multimedia constructs have long been a part of gallery-level exhibitions, and the visual concepts supplied by games have been embraced by dozens of contemporary artists. But games and art nevertheless maintain an uneasy relationship. And in my opinion, the question of whether games themselves can be art in the same way that, say, sculpture and portraiture can occasionally overshadows the fact that games are used by people like Condon for highly creative and innovative purposes. This question has generated long, overwrought, often tortuous debate and has been hotly contested by gamers, academics, and critics of all kinds. Like the value of games generally, the value of games as art is indistinct, unresolved, and notoriously messy.

Once again the thoughts of Professor Henry Jenkins are illuminating, this time on the subject of why games have had to struggle for the same status as other expressive media: "We might ask where the resistance is coming from. It is coming from partisans of other arts. It comes from film critics who are worried that their preferred medium is going to be superseded. It is coming from literary critics who are concerned that young people are playing games rather than reading books. It comes from those whose notion of art is so narrow that very few works qualify, as opposed to those of us who have a fairly expansive notion of art and are willing to welcome in new aesthetic experiences. It comes from gamers who worry that calling games art means that they are going to become too obscure and pretentious (small danger there, guys). It has to do with our totally messed up notion of what constitutes art."

For the purposes of this text, I think that the issue of whether games constitute art can be safely ignored. I think this partly because there are so many other reasons to value games and partly because, as Condon insists, "the question of what is considered art (or not art) hasn't been relevant since 1929, when Duchamp put a urinal on the wall." Condon argues: "It is about context. Call it art, whatever it is, and I will accept it and will discuss it as such." I feel the same way.

The reason for arguing that games—at least some games—deserve to be classified as art is that it offers gamers a more positive, culturally sanctioned way to describe what they do. It suggests that games are not mere trivia. It also enables us to place a higher value on—to elevate—what game developers do. Just as the term *art* suggests that strolling through a gallery isn't just time spent staring at passing walls, it would also suggest that gaming involves more than twitching in front of a monitor.

## GHOST PATTERNS

Games—like films, books, sports, and other cultural activities—cater to deep emotional, intellectual, and sensual needs. Gamers buy games not simply because they're fine pieces of art or even well-programmed pieces of software but because they produce significant physical and emotional responses. The abstract satisfaction of deleting a row of *Tetris* blocks, the heart-quickening thrill of a snowboarding simulation—these are the reasons we play games. The responses produced by games vary endlessly in their qualities, but their existence and their significance is undeniable. My task, and the task that others have begun to take upon themselves, is to find out what value the responses that games produce in us really have. How do games affect us? How does playing a video game change the person who plays it?

Steven Johnson's popular book-length thought experiment *Everything Bad Is Good for You* begins its exploration of the beneficial effects of playing games by pointing out that games, far from being slothful indulgence, are usually formidable undertakings. "The first and last thing that should be said about the experience of playing today's video games, the thing that you almost never hear in mainstream coverage, is that games are fiendishly, sometimes maddeningly, *hard.*" Johnson spotted what I knew from playing *Quake III,* which is that games present us with unusual, often intractable problems. We do not sit back in our armchairs and passively digest them—we puzzle over them, wrestle with them, and defeat them.

The intellectual value of video games, Johnson argues, has to do with the fact that they aren't explicit about their rules. Unlike a traditional game, such as chess, where the rules are fully spelled out in advance, you have to uncover the rules of individual video games as you go along. Most computer games are nonexplicit "fuzzy" experiences. "You have to probe the depths of the game's logic to make sense of it," says Johnson, "and like most probing expeditions you get results by trial and error, by stumbling across things, by following hunches." Johnson suggests that this process of "probing" is a complex learned activity that is analogous to the scientific method. This assertion is seconded by Professor Stephen Heppell of the University of East Anglia, who writes in "Unlimited Learning": "My own research work has revealed that a very clear set of strategies has evolved by children playing computer games. To succeed in even the simplest platform game, children have to lock their problem solving into a tight cycle of observe, question, hypothesize, test. Curiously, this exactly matches the scientific method that education has been trying to embed in young scientists since the birth of science."

Video games are more about how you play them than about their fancy explosions or even their characters and stories. What motivates the mushroom people is infinitely less important than learning how to run, jump, and open treasure chests. During video game play, we engage in processes of gradual, often rather complex experimentation. These processes uncover rules about the game world that we can use again in other situations. The players who realized that every firearm recoil pattern in the game *Counter-Strike* was the same suddenly had a supernatural understanding of the physics of their game world: what should have been random suddenly had a pattern that could be understood and predicted. Every single round from an automatic weapon could be anticipated.

However, unlike the scientific method, much of what gamers learn is outside conscious awareness. As we play, we internalize various rules and discover methods, often relying on them because they occasionally reap rewards or because they just happen to feel like the right thing to do in the game world. Thanks to months of playing *Quake III*, I learned instinctively that by hitting certain keys as my *Quake* character jumped, I could travel farther. As it happened, this had been specifically designed into the game, but I only realized I was doing it when, months later, I read about the concept of "strafe jumping." Someone else, long before, realized he could get to a high ledge by jumping on the explosion from a rocket. The blast wouldn't be enough to kill him, but the inertia would be enough to propel him higher and faster than mere leaping. This technique now arrives almost subliminally for *Quake* players, but rocket jumping has long been recognized as one of *Quake*'s key skills.

Another example of unconscious, practical learning from *Quake* is that of leading your shots. When playing in an online game, the signal from your "snapshot" of the game has to bounce from your computer to the remote computer on which the gaming is being hosted and back again. This means that where your game draws your enemy and where the server thinks he is might be slightly out of sync. Shooting slightly ahead of where you see him allows players to counter that. Many *Quake* players learned to do this without even being able to explicitly identify it as a tactic. It simply felt right.

Of course, there is also the potential for something more complicated, beyond "probing" and beyond unconscious mastery of a gun that shoots lightning bolts. This is a process that Steven Johnson defines as "telescoping." Telescoping refers to the way that gamers have to deal with multiple objectives, each one resting inside the next like the concentric rings in a telescope. Johnson uses the example of a *Zelda* game in which the ultimate objective is to rescue your sister. To complete this core objective, players engage in continuous management of layer after layer of secondary and tertiary objectives. Each one must be completed before other tasks are possible. For Link, the main character in *Zelda*, killing an enemy so that he can cross a bridge requires that he have a weapon. Having a weapon requires that he complete the weapon quest, completing the weapon quest means speaking to the fairy, speaking to the fairy means accessing the map, and so on and so forth. Gamers have to be able to juggle all this and understand which objectives to sideline and when to do so, if they are to get closer to their overall goal. Johnson's thesis is that this kind of layered play develops our abilities to cope with the chaotic storm of information that constitutes modern living. Games are so hard, so complex, that we reap huge cognitive rewards by learning to overcome them. "Information overload" isn't such a problem for those people who have taken lessons from gaming, says Johnson.

A growing body of scientific study supports Johnson's claims. A report published in October 2006 by the Federation of American Scientists (FAS) concluded that contemporary educational systems lacked the capacity to assess the kinds of skills that video games taught, meaning that they ultimately went undetected. Additionally, the FAS paper concluded: "Video game developers have instinctively implemented many of the common axioms of learning scientists. They have used these approaches to help game players exercise a skill set closely matching the thinking, planning, learning, and technical skills increasingly demanded by employers in a wide range of industries."

The range of cognitive skills found to benefit from time spent gaming continues to widen. Researchers at the University of Rochester in New York have been examining the plasticity of human visual processing by using video gamers as test subjects. The Rochester team wanted to see whether habitual game playing improved visual skills, and their report explained that "video game players were found to outperform non-video game players on the localization of an eccentric target among distractors, on the number of visual items they could apprehend at once, and on the fast temporal processing of visual information." This kind of research—the cognitive neuroscience of video games—has only recently been undertaken, but it is nevertheless a rapidly expanding subject. The work so far performed in the field has consistently demonstrated that habitual gamers tend to have improved spatial cognitive skills, enhanced visual attention, and the ability to process multiple tasks with greater efficiency. Games, it seems, change gamers' brains for the better.

## NINTENDO SURGEON

It seems that gamers are learning new techniques for managing information. Academic studies have begun to illustrate that video game principles go hand in hand with new ways of learning. The Entertainment and Leisure Software Publishers Association (ELSPA) wants to show us that games can help in other, more formal places, too—particularly in schools.

ELSPA has made numerous attempts to provide due credit for the activities of its members. An example of this is their 2006 paper "Unlimited Learning," which set out to highlight how games fit into the overall process of learning and education in schools. The paper lists dozens of examples in which games have been used as teaching aids and learning tools. It shows that games give us the capacity to teach in ways that were previously out of reach. We could imagine, for example, a board game or pen-and-paper role-playing games based on running a school, but when you add to this a computer, 3-D planning systems, and the ability to control real-time calculations of costs as they will be encountered in the real world, you suddenly have something both accessible to children and complex enough to teach adult ideas.

One U.K. school, in Birmingham, opted for an approach that melded exactly these kinds of ideas. A contributor to the ELSPA report explained how it worked: "We were originally going to use *SimCity 4* but thought it too detailed for the 1.5 hours we had the children. *School Tycoon* [a commercial product] allowed us to get the children to develop their spatial thinking skills, fiscal skills, numeracy, and even social awareness. Many did not realize the jobs that are entailed in running a school and how essential they are. The pupils were given cards to make their own 'physical' school within a budget and were then shown the software. They were allowed to play in the 'sandbox' mode for an hour and then we print-screened the final school with financial and academic results to determine who had been successful." Approaches like the *School Tycoon* project allow students to benefit from the graphic, illustrative qualities of gaming systems, while at the same time learning to work with physical models and practical mathematical systems. Better still, being good with games is something that kids want to demonstrate to their peers.

Another teacher, Tim Rylands, used an adapted version of the game *Myst* as a teaching aid in classes of children

7–11 years old. The game improved literacy because of its text focus and its comparative "cool." The appeal of playing a video game to the children meant that they maintained attention longer than they would have done with a book, even though the amount of text delivered was similar. Using the game also had other social effects for the class, because it was played by committee rather than through solo decision making. One of the students had this to say about her experience: "The most difficult thing about using *Myst* at first was having to make decisions as a group to solve the problems. We needed to learn a lot of negotiation skills so that we could work our way towards the solutions together. It's fun to talk about where you have got up to in the game and how to solve different problems." In this case, gaming was not simply a cognitive exercise or cerebral puzzle, it was a social conundrum that children were forced to resolve through discussion and cooperation.

In many ways, of course, these examples are really nothing new. We've known for a long time that the process of play is crucial to the development of all greater mammals, particularly humans. Studies with developing animals have consistently shown that creatures who have been deprived of suitable play suffer from developmental problems. Psychologist Diane Ackerman's 2000 book on the development of human beings, *Deep Play,* has this to say about our most vital method of learning: "Play is an activity enjoyed for its own sake. It is our brain's favorite way of learning and maneuvering. Because we think of play as the opposite of seriousness, we don't notice that it governs most of society. . . . even in its least intoxicating forms, play feels satisfying, absorbing, and has rules and a life of its own, while offering rare challenges. It is organic to who and what we are, a process as instinctive as breathing." We learn through infantile roughhousing, we learn through adventures with our toys, and some of us learned secondary-level French by playing pirated adventure games. Whatever the particulars, there's no way to deny its significance. Video games are rapidly becoming a dominant and useful form of play: now we have to understand why that is and what it means.

If schoolchildren can learn from the inherent playfulness of video games, then so, surely, can U.S. marines. In early 2006, the University of California's Information Sciences Institute developed a learning suite called *Tactical Iraqi*, with the aim of teaching soldiers how to interact successfully with Iraqi civilians. The system was based on familiar video game conventions: a first-person point of view, a menu of options for character behavior, and so on. The system taught spoken as well as body language, allowing soldiers to experiment in a safe environment and learn the best way to approach social situations with the people they were going to be policing on a daily basis. Allowing soldiers to work and practice at their own computer terminal wasn't just convenient for military instructors, it was also (reportedly) intuitive to a generation of soldiers who had grown up with video games.

The U.S. military has explained that video games were "necessary and natural" for training. Nevertheless, there is no evidence whatsoever that games have a causal link to violence or that gamers are less inhibited about using weapons, as some U.S. military officials have suggested. All such claims have, so far, been groundless and often transparently motivated by ulterior concerns. (I'm a *Quake* genius and I can't hit a clay pigeon with a 12 gauge.) Personally, I regard projects like *Tactical Iraqi* as positive for gamers, even if the politics of that particular project seem dubious and even if military officials do harbor hopes that games will teach their charges how to destroy people with multimillion-dollar attack helicopters.

I do not want to diminish the idea that games are good for hand-eye coordination. There are plenty of reasons to believe that playing video games increases proficiency with technological interfaces and improves general "twitch" skills, and the importance of this should not be understated. Our interaction with electronic and mechanical devices becomes ever more important as the technological level of society rises. One crucial example of the relation of games to this phenomenon comes from the work performed by New York surgeon Dr. James Rosser. An exponent of "minimally invasive surgery" and an experienced medical practitioner, Rosser seems about as far from artist Brody Condon as you might care to imagine. Yet both are gamers who have made something positive from their time spent with games. Both men have applied what they learned from games to their professional lives. Games helped Condon find his mode of artistic expression; Rosser used them to improve the coordination and dexterity of his trainee surgeons. Rosser insists that playing on a Nintendo console is as essential a part of the success of his Top Gun training program as more traditional exercises. Surgeons who played at least three hours of *Super Monkey Ball* each week made 37 percent fewer errors, according to Rosser. Games weren't optional or trivial for this surgeon: they were mandatory. "You have to be a Nintendo surgeon," he told *Wired* magazine.

THE ELECTRONIC ANTIDOTE

Computerization has transformed our idea of what constitutes a game. The Copenhagen-based gaming academic Jesper Juul argues that the computer stands to the medium of gaming as the printing press stands to the medium of writing. Until the printing press was invented, the written word only had a limited set of applications; likewise, games were previously limited to boards, cards, or verbal play. Now, thanks to computing technologies, their application and potential seems unlimited, and they could scarcely be more different in their content and themes: contrast *Robotron* and *Oblivion* or *Second Life* and *Blast Corps*. Video games represent a previously unimagined terrain for play, one that is almost impossible to survey with any authority. A critic of games journalism recently asked, "Where is the Lester Bangs of games journalism?" And a chorus of gamers responded, "Where is the man who has time to play even a fraction of the games out there?" In just 40 years, the concept of gaming has exploded into a wide palette of gaming experience. The possibilities for play—and learning through play—are gradually opening up new ground (as well as meticulously retreading successful ideas over and over). They are also ushering in some pleasing, constructive trends. Still, I am far from thinking that laudable ends, such as learning and education, are the most important possibilities that have been opened up by the proliferation and evolution of gaming. In fact, though those are positive things, what is most valuable to me about computerized play is the fact that it offers new and far greater possibilities for being entertained.

This claim, of course, brings us full circle back to a more conventional idea of what games are: namely, that they're fun ways to pass time. Sure, they improve reaction-based skills—skills that are often transferable and demonstrable, as Dr. Rosser believes them to be. And they might just make us better soldiers or students. But that's not their main function. In some cases, they might even make us smarter, as Steven Johnson suggests, by improving such cognitive skills as information handling and problem solving. But let's not lose sight of their core value: games are an antidote to boredom, an excellent cure for a seriously debilitating malaise.

I believe that boredom is a far greater problem than most people are willing to acknowledge. This lack of acknowledgment may reflect the fact that boredom is so closely associated with idleness that many people find it hard to believe that someone might be bored for legitimate reasons. Boredom is frequently dismissed as a personal failing. But that's simply not the case. Boredom is often a result of circumstance rather than a general lack of enterprise. A person will often be bored by something. We often find ourselves at a motivational loss or without the means to keep our minds suitably occupied—think of the importance of a toy to a child whose family is visiting the antique realm of an elderly relative or the significance of a book or mobile phone when stranded in the experiential desert of an international airport. We all experience boredom at some time or other, although some of us are more resistant to it than others. It seems safe to say that avoiding boredom is important to almost everyone, and some of us have developed complex strategies for expunging it completely. Perhaps one of the crucial reasons why boredom is so ignored is that it is gone and forgotten when it is resolved. Unlike melancholy or alienation, boredom is utterly transient and intangible. It is so nebulous and vague that philosophers and psychologists despair of coming to grips with it in any meaningful or helpful way.

My personal familiarity with the agonies of boredom drove me to think about it in more depth, but I initially understood little about the condition. Boredom remains elusive to almost anyone you might talk to—even the literature of boredom is notably uninformative and thin. Most of my own understanding of it derives from a book called *A Philosophy of Boredom,* by the Norwegian philosophy professor

Lars Svendsen. This unassuming little tome, first published in 2005, strikes deep at the heart of the concept, identifying trends within boredom, strains of boredom, and the relationship between boredom and modern life. Until you take some time to consider boredom as a significant and complex subject, as Svendsen does, it might not seem particularly significant. The more we delve, however, the more we see how broad the problem is. Svendsen, too, notes that boredom is one of the least well-studied aspects of human life, despite widespread reference to its consequences throughout philosophy and literature. Being less romantic than other maladies of the soul, boredom has been relatively neglected by humanists and scientists.

What is clear is that use of the term *boredom* has increased ceaselessly since the eighteenth century. It cannot be found in English before 1760, and although Svendsen notes that some European languages came up with equivalent words in the centuries before, they were generally derivations of the Latin for "hate" and carried similar meanings. Usage of the term in its contemporary sense nevertheless increased steadily from the late eighteenth century, and by 1932, boredom had come to denote something genuinely worth worrying about, as Svendsen cites Bertrand Russell's thoughts on the matter: "Boredom as a factor in human behavior has received, in my opinion, far less attention than it deserves. It has, I believe, been one of the motive powers through the historical epoch, and it is so at the present day more than ever." Boredom, it seems, is not a new problem, but it is one of peculiar concern to modern humans.

Svendsen also quotes Fernando Pessoa, who identifies boredom as "the feeling that there's nothing worth doing." The bored are those people for whom no activity seems satisfactory. The problem is often not that there is a lack of things to do in general but, rather, that there is a lack of things that are worthwhile. Boredom can arise in all kinds of situations, but it usually makes itself known when we cannot do what we want to do or when we must do something we do not wish to do or something we cannot find a satisfactory reason for. "Boredom is not a question of idleness," suggests Svendsen, "but of meaning." Boredom does not, however, equate to the kind of meaninglessness found in depression. The bored are not necessarily unhappy with life; they are simply unfulfilled by circumstances, activities, and the things around them.

In my experience, gamers are rarely bored when they have access to their hobby. (And many are deeply bored when disconnected from it.) Obviously games do not provide a solution for everyone, but could they be the gamer's antidote to boredom and therefore meaninglessness? Could the end-in-itself of mastering *Pac-Man* or *Secret Of Mana* be enough to banish the curse of boredom from our lives? And does that imply that games provide us with a distinct value? In a world where so many of us feel bored and alienated from our jobs, could games provide a special kind of amusement, one that instantly dissolves the memory of office-bound tedium? Are these fantasy projects really just as good as anything else—books, art, team sports, study, politics—that might fill out lives? Are the small victories in digital worlds really enough to keep the gray blankness of boredom at bay? "Leisure is in itself no more meaningful than work," says Svendsen. "The basic question is how one chooses to be idle." For those of us who choose video games, "idleness" can seem extremely satisfying, although we're seldom idle in any obvious sense. Games are hives of activity. A few hours spent defeating puzzles in *Mario Sunshine* (often passing the controller back and forth between my partner and myself) seems just as fulfilling as most other leisure activities and happily balloons to fill almost any length of time you might imagine. Games are often dismissed as a timesink that makes us oblivious to the passing of the hours—but that's part of the reason we play them, and it is, in my opinion, a very good thing.

It is not a coincidence that video games now comprise some of the most sophisticated and expensive technologies in the world. We have plowed countless millions of dollars into developing these electronic systems, and only a fraction of it is done for purely commercial reasons. The other motivation—amusement—is far more powerful. Gaming has claimed a huge stake in our culture, especially if you define culture as the time we spend on doing things that we don't have to do. And it is not chance that our digital entertainments are so complex and demanding. Getting to the end of *Space Tripper* or completing *Resident Evil 4* are hardly trivial undertakings, and it says something about our desperation to sidestep boredom that so many tens of thousands of people have worked their way up to level 60 (or 70) in *World of Warcraft*.

Games represent a uniquely modern response to the proliferating phenomenon of boredom. Games are an electronic antidote to the chronic condition prophesied by Londoner and author J. G. Ballard: "I would sum up my fear about the future in one word: boring. And that's my one fear: that everything has happened; nothing exciting or new or interesting is ever going to happen again. . . . the future is just going to be a vast, conforming suburb of the soul." Ballard's fiction is famous for exploring the idea that humans might end up resorting to psychopathic acts to escape this "suburb of the soul." He sees the homogenous and commercialized future as a bleak one, filled with Svendsen's boredom-through-meaninglessness. But my aim here is to show that we have rather less destructive solutions at hand for diverting such a bleak future—tools for play; engines for novelty and thrill, expression and exploration. Take time to examine a cross section of video games and you'll encounter grand life simulations, blistering fictive racing experiments, ultradetailed management tools, savage retina-roasting fractal spectra, pet dogs, Escher physics, digital cooking competitions, boundless horror, and impossible geographies. Even if you don't share the bleak outlook of soothsayers like Ballard, video games still represent a fascinating, ostentatious landscape of experiences that were not previously available to us. Perhaps we have boredom to thank for that.

The differences between genres of games are now so startling that commentators often struggle with the label of "game" when attempting to describe them. Contrast the players who puzzle through *Tetris* to the *Second Life* denizens who run businesses in virtual worlds. Contrast people jigging on dance mats to the long, slow precipitation of planning in a game of *SimCity*. Contrast my 40 minutes of absolute reptilian-response engagement in a game of *Quake* to a *World of Warcraft* player harvesting herbs to make a magic potion. The differences, the experiential wealth of gaming, makes it tough to describe and even harder to survey, but the games do all have one thing in common: for minutes, hours, weeks, months, and years of our lives, games defeat boredom.

In his 2006 essay "The Space to Play," the Nokia futurologist Matt Jones considered the issues of play and gaming from the point of view of a designer and technological speculator. Jones wanted to show how designers could learn from activities like gaming to make their products more intuitive and more engaging. In so doing, he highlighted the psychological concept of "flow." Jones explains: "Whether thrilling or relaxing, one thing that games designers can teach those wrestling with other more general forms of interaction design is a mastery of 'flow.' Identified by psychologist Mihaly Csikszentmihalyi, flow in human experience 'is a mental state of operation in which the person is fully immersed in what he or she is doing, characterized by a feeling of energized focus, full involvement, and success in the process of the activity' (to use the Wikipedia definition). Flow and play are inextricable—Csikszentmihalyi refers to the 'playground' environment necessary to attain a flow state, and the balance of challenge and ability that governs the flow state is essential to the sustenance of good play."

The flow state is familiar to all gamers (the slang reference is something like "being in the zone"), and it was the main reason why I was obsessed with *Quake III*. Running the team and my subsequent lifestyle changes were means to the perfect moments of electronic combat, the feeling of control and precision, the awareness of flow. The same thing can, of course, be true of driving a car, having an excellent conversation, or being immersed in writing. But the extent to which our experience of games is an experience of psychological flow goes some way to explaining why we value it. And in my opinion, this experience is more than enough. Notwithstanding all the other ways games might change us, all the improvements to cognitive skills, social well-being, and welfare they can offer, the best—and ultimately only necessary—defense of games is that they keep us engaged and entertained. From extended engagement in hypnotic pattern completion to punctuated moments of joy in victory, we get something from gaming that feels important. As games proliferate and become still more sophisticated, we may well find that the Ballardian idea of the future as inevitably boring becomes unthinkable. Gamers, I think, are already there.

# The Big Smoke

It's July 2007, and Southern England is being gradually submerged in the heaviest rains for 60 years. Intercity trains to and from the West Country, where I live, are forced to roll slowly through shallow lakes of water (a scene reminiscent of a drab, burned-out version of the end of the animated film *Spirited Away*). Half the London Underground is closed due to flooding, and I must take a circuitous, oversubscribed subway route to reach my destination, Victoria Station. The familiar central London travel hub is awash with water from the leaking roof. Hundreds of people stand about forlornly staring at the departure boards. Most trains out of the station have been canceled.

I'm going to be late for my meeting with an old *Quake* acquaintance, Paul "Locki" Wedgwood, who has long been a key member of the British and European *Quake III* community. As a key organizational gamer, he was responsible for rallying my team to exhibition matches, and although we did not meet until many years later, we corresponded regularly around these events. Very occasionally, we even played in the same games.

"Locki" was a regular name on the *Quake* chat channels, and he managed to drum up plenty of support for the game and its variants on U.K. game services. The success of my team and dozens of others depended on people like Wedgwood running the community—delivering news, organizing competitions, and making sure servers stayed online. Their dedication meant the games were free and well maintained.

These days, however, Wedgwood's interest in the *Quake* community is altogether more serious: he's making the games that these online communities will play. Wedgwood is now the owner of Splash Damage, which is working with id Software and Activision to make *Enemy Territory: Quake Wars.* (By the time you read this, *Quake Wars* will have been played by tens of thousands of gamers across the world. At the time I was traveling through London, however, almost no one had played the game, and it was a largely unknown quantity—just another work in progress.) This sequel to both *Quake* and *Return to Castle Wolfenstein*'s free *Enemy Territory* expansion will be one of the major games of 2007. It's a first-person online shooter, like *Quake III,* in which gamers take up the roles of human defenders and alien invaders on a lavish futuristic battlefield. Given its pedigree, I'm boyishly excited about being able to play it for the first time. The flood-driven delays and the slowly trundling train I finally catch from Victoria combine in a nexus of frustration and make me want to scream. I regret not bringing a thicker book with me to read.

When I finally step into Splash Damage's offices (over the pallet bridge across voluminous puddles), Wedgwood doesn't seem to notice my tardiness. He's all smiles. With glasses, goatee, black Splash Damage T-shirt, and a collection of sci-fi figurines around the windows of the demo room, he fulfills plenty of familiar gamer traits. But there's something else detectable in him: a glint in the eye, a strong sense of just how focused and dedicated he has become. He's a man who understands his mission. Video games have changed Wedgwood, and he knows it. More than that, he embraces it. Like so many other people I meet in London, Wedgwood is someone for whom games have become the currency of his life.

Wedgwood has been prodigiously successful, not only in creating a major game but in getting into a position of corporately funded creativity by virtue of his own passion for gaming. It's fair to say that he's one of London's most accomplished gamers. *Quake Wars* may have been a massive project involving dozens of people and millions of dollars, but it was Wedgwood's baby. He's plugged into every aspect of it, and his face lights up with a mixture of pride, delight, and obsession as he demonstrates the game to me. He talks at speed, leaping from one subject to the next with alarming energy. He talks as one gamer does to another, with only the most minor inflections of marketingspeak creeping into his monologue. He stops and apologizes for talking in what he calls "salespeak," explaining that he has trained himself to trot off accolades and financial factoids so that he can sell the game to distributors and retail reps. Getting the message across to the nongamers, especially these money men, has become a full-time job. I confirm that I understand, and we continue.

There must be hundreds of men like Wedgwood across Greater London—men for whom gaming has become the great escape. They've all come to games out of a desire for leisure-time distractions, but some, like Wedgwood and his colleagues, take it much further. In fact, on reflection, Wedgwood has probably taken his gaming further than any of the gamers I've met in the past decade. He has been utterly faithful to his obsession, and it has been faithful to him. He started off, like me, by finding a *Quake* team in the late 1990s—one of the European "clans" of *Team Fortress* and *Quake* players—and playing routinely. His competitive nature shone through as the team began to win on a routine basis. Wedgwood led from the front, as he has continued to do throughout his career in games. As he played more and more, he began to forge strong links with the people who made up the online community. More important, he had time to sink into writing news and running game Web sites. "I got a job as a contract IT guy in a bank in the City," he explained in an interview we'd done a few months earlier. "Because it had trading floors, I wasn't allowed to touch the network between nine and five. So my job was to sit at my desk and not touch anything. Instead of actually doing anything, I spent most of 1998 updating the *Team Fortress* news desk." Suddenly he had a second job, and rather than dwelling on the lonely existence of a server administrator, he began to connect with a young, energetic community.

As Wedgwood became increasingly integrated in the gaming community, he began to get involved with the now-defunct gaming community service Barrysworld. At the same time, however, his work began to suffer. Like me, he'd found something more important. He soon lost his job at the bank and then another working for a government tech department. After months of chatting and gaming with the folks who ran the Barrysworld service, Wedgwood discovered that its chairman lived just a few blocks away in the same part of London. The two men arranged to meet for a drink, and soon Wedgwood was filling the role of infrastructure manager for the gaming service. "It was a big pay cut," Wedgwood explained. "But by then I knew I had to be in the games industry."

After a month of the familiar routine of commissioning servers and dealing with the technical issues of Internet gaming, Wedgwood found himself commentating on *Quake* matches that were to be televised on Now TV, a cable channel that was selling content into the Asian market. All the action took place during unsociable hours—weekends, evenings, and so on. "So during the week," he explained, "I got more and more involved in mod work." *Mod work,* or *modding,* is the process of taking an existing game and modifying it to create free variants. It's a kind of nonprofit amateur game design. It was to be the foundation of what Wedgwood and his allies would do with the commercial *Quake Wars* project. "*Team Fortress* had been the main thing for us, but we were all looking forward to *Quake III.* I joined up with a mod team called *Q3F,* based on *Fortress,* and I soon became project leader for this *Quake III* mod."

This was the crucial turning point for Wedgwood. By taking up modification, Wedgwood had set out not to make a game from scratch but, instead, to build something based on a work undertaken by a professional team. By standing on the shoulders of giants and repurposing what had gone before, Wedgwood could create something new and viable. In this case, it was a modification of *Quake III,* but Wedgwood could have chosen any number of commercial games. What was most significant about modding projects like this, however, was that it demonstrated that games were entering a new era and taking gamers with them. Wedgwood was working with a team that was based across Europe and getting help from game designers in Dallas in a project that would be the foundation for a new career in game development. His story was fascinating to me because it seemed to exemplify what so much coverage of the gaming press missed out on: how games were influencing the lives of the people who played them. It was becoming clear from my visits to London that they were influencing many, many people.

Wedgwood's London was becoming another node in an international, globalized gaming culture. He and his team are representative of this latest phase of British gaming—one that is heavily influenced by American and Japanese game design but has also hooked itself up to an evolving, networked culture. The entire Splash Damage team were inspired by and connected via the Internet, and the game development—the modification—that they immersed themselves in was very different from the amateur games environment that had previously existed in the United Kingdom. Fifteen or twenty years earlier, homes across Britain were nurturing a generation of game designers whose experiences with games were rather unlike those of Wedgwood's team. This was once a nation of "bedroom programmers," a phenomenon of one- or two-man game design teams, facilitated by the simplicity of the 8-bit (and then 16-bit) home computers that proliferated at the end of the 1980s. The British games industry thrived in those years thanks to the sheer number of home computers and the creativity they engendered. While the rest of the world was falling into the thrall of Atari, Nintendo, and then Sega, Britain's gaming language was being written in machine code on ZX Spectrums and Commodore Amigas. Game design was rampant, weird, and wonderful. The country produced both defining video games and a generation of gamers whose experience of making their own games was at odds with the way games are made today—in multimillion-dollar media studios across the world. Many Britons see that era of early home computing as a golden age of gaming. It was a time in which anyone could get involved in the process of making games. Copying a few lines out of a manual or learning a crude programming language was all it took to start making games. Almost everyone had access to the tools—home computing was cheap and ubiquitous;

creativity was unbounded. Many of the principles of games as they are seen today were conceived and delivered in that neolithic era of computerized play.

The home-programming culture has now largely been lost, thanks to the increasing complexity and commercialization of gaming. There's a pocket of personal creativity here and there (the British company Introversion springs to mind), but to create games now means raising large budgets and employing dozens of professionals, exactly as Wedgwood does in his South London studio. But Wedgwood's project also demonstrates that there is still hope for individuals wanting to find their way in. Thanks to the tools and the technological scaffolding provided by modding, the bedroom programmers do still have a way of making something unique—even if it means working with others across the Net. In Wedgwood's era, creativity is once again being facilitated by cheap computers and simple tools, but these are tools provided by the commercial games industry and distributed electronically.

Modifying games has become both the new amateur art form that could drive the creation of games onward and upward and the training grounds for potential commercial game creators. It's not the only way of making amateur games—and the programming of one person can still achieve a great deal—but it is a new way, one that has had major ramifications for many of the gamers I have encountered. It makes the creation of games accessible to all—not just the gilded elite.

Where once Britain was a nation of solitary programmers, it is now a node in an international network of cut-and-paste video game creation—a place where gamers can get a leg up from the efforts of the professionals and create professional-looking games via a series of shortcuts. Modding games, I will later argue, is one of the ways in which gaming will begin to change gamers' lives all over again. We'll come back to Wedgwood and his companions later, as I discuss just how gamers have been inspired to change the medium in which they live and play.

## LIVING INSTANCES

Let's now leave me goggle-eyed in front of that first session of *Quake Wars* and roll back a few years to the time that followed my stint as a financial journalist (and consequently my most excruciating encounters with boredom). Back then I thought of London as a city of toil, depression, and long journeys spent jostling with exhausted commuters. I moved away to a cheerily provincial tourist trap of a town in the West Country of England, where I sit writing these words today. I was glad to see the back of the big city, and several times I turned down job offers that would have meant returning there. But soon my idea of London began to change. As my new career developed, I began to journey to London and greet the people I met there with a new perspective. The people I now traveled to London to see (people like Wedgwood) were illustrative of how and why my life had gone down the route it had. London became the place I went to in order to talk to interesting gamers—gamers who talk about *SingStar, Tekken,* or *Project: Ico* with wide eyes or razor-sharp sarcasm; gamers who are jet-lagged and still pumping with adrenaline from a weeklong gaming competition in Korea; gamers who are bitter about the loss of their "golden age" or thrilled by unforeseen developments. These knowledgeable, energetic people, who have things to say and insights to share, replaced the financiers and clerks of my previous life. These gamers were living instances of how games had changed people's lives and how games had changed my life. Their enthusiasm was infectious, galvanizing.

My travels had begun to reveal that almost all writing and reporting concerned with gaming overlooked what the experience of gaming had meant to the gamers themselves. There was some talk about the intellectual or cognitive experience, but how games slotted into different lives and how they changed perceptions and agendas was being ignored. Most writing about games was about "the product" or about some particular phenomenon—virtual economies, violence in games, marriage via *EverQuest*. But there was more to it than that: I wanted to talk about what the gamers themselves were doing, to describe about what they were like and how the experience of gaming manifested itself in their different lives. How does that Saturday afternoon spent smashing cars in *Crackdown* fit into the life of a dedicated father and accountant? How are schoolchildren's personal politics influenced by educational games? How have South Korean youngsters turned avoiding boredom into a profession? The need to talk about these things was what made the present writing possible.

Take, for example, a man called Jonathan Smith. I encounter Smith on an irregular basis, each time bumping into him at a different stage in his career in games—here in an Internet café in central London, there at the Olympia convention center—each time with a different game-related theme. Smith had, I learned, once worked on the same magazine that had saved me from unemployment. Long before my time, he had moved on to write a book, to work on video games, to get a job with Lego, and eventually to found his own company. In 2006 I was sent on an assignment to see this new company and talk to its creative director.

I arrived at Smith's far-periphery-of-London headquarters (on the outskirts of the conurbation somewhere near the Chilterns) on a mild summer afternoon. We had arranged the details of the meeting a couple of months previously in a hired barroom packed with bloggers and folk from the games industry—unshaven men who stood around drinking beer and trying not to talk about games—and so the venue for this latest meeting couldn't have been more different. Set in a large, modestly maintained garden, the large Victorian house was unlike any other development office I had visited. It was a whole world of domesticity and languid porch-dwelling cats away from the sequence of downtown studios on office blocks I had reported on across the world. Smith's office was situated in a small building on the grounds of the main house. He led the way down a gravel driveway of what was a very English home. It was the nerve center of development for the sequel to 2005's most successful British video game, *Lego Star Wars*, which sold three and a half million copies its first year. "Of course, there are still offices where the work happens," Smith explained as we entered the kitchen-office area to make a cup of tea and a sandwich. "Traveller's Tales [the main studio] have about a hundred people in Manchester." In that cottage just outside Burnham (a suburban appendix to the concrete jungles of Slough), Smith and the company director, Tom Stone, along with their lead producers and the Q & A team (secreted upstairs in the cottage bedrooms), were working toward making the perfect sequel to the previous year's success.

Smith sat down in a large, well-upholstered armchair to tell me about the relationship he had created between several different game companies. His own small production unit had to work with the larger development studio (Traveller's Tales) as well as Lego, the publishers at Activision, and the *Star Wars* franchise controllers at LucasArts. "It's a relationship of love," Smith laughed. "Everyone has input onto what the game should be, so it's never a forced marriage." Smith is one of a small cadre of gamer-developers who seem to have exact control over their passion for gaming. The results of this focused energy have meant that the people who work around Smith display enormous trust in his abilities to create a worthwhile game. One of his team confided in me that he was amazed by Smith's insight and long-term enthusiasm for the medium. They were traits I had seen many times in people who were gamers long before they were industry professionals.

The fact that both Activision and LucasArts (two games industry monoliths) were now so interested in the *Lego Star Wars* concept seemed like a reflection of Smith's honed gaming instincts. People had been uncertain about the idea of fusing *Star Wars* with Lego, but that kind of doubt hadn't been an issue for Smith. His time working at Lego had been revelatory, and he articulated some of that effect on him. He talked about being "immersed in toys" and explained that the attitude Lego had toward their "play materials" (the plastic kits) had gone a long way toward expanding his own understanding of what it is to play. For someone who had been around gaming for decades, it seemed like a period of refreshment and enlightenment. "Play has many meanings and its own semantics. Lego was about nothing less than fun," said Smith. "And that's not mere corporate gobbledygook. To be immersed in that and tasked with finding out what games Lego could make was liberating. We meshed that with our own commercial awareness, so it wasn't just R & D. It was about making something that kids would love to play with." But, more important, Smith was, for the first time, really set on making something that everyone could enjoy.

"We knew we had what it took to express Lego interac-

tively," said Smith, although the expression of plastic toy in
sci-fi video game was clearly never a straightforward problem. "There was a big challenge in making the minifigure
into a video game character. Animating them makes a video
game character, but it has to be done in a way that makes
them a video game and not a simulation." Watching Smith
steer Princess Leia's chunky legs around the screen suggested that there was as much inspiration as perspiration
in making that happen. This idea of his game not being a
simulation was important to Smith. *Lego Star Wars* was
about playing, not about building. It was not an attempt to
simulate Lego itself. "It's not a 'CAD' experience," said
Smith, when I ask him why there's no "real" building in
*Lego Star Wars* but, rather, a series of puzzles in which
pieces assemble themselves. "It's not a simulation of the
plastic Lego experience—it's the imaginative exercise. It's
exploration. Lego translates differently into the video game
space. It's not about building, because that becomes frus-
trating. Of course, you can mix things up in the game
world, but not in the same way as the real world."

This was where Smith's philosophy as a gamer became
apparent: "We are delivering imagination and not simulation." You can see these aspects of Smith's attitude emerging within the game: there's a constant two-player dynamic,
where someone can drop in and join the first player at any
moment—someone like a busy parent. Smith says, quite seriously, that he thinks the Lego games are "for the child in
all of us." It's clear that his project is motivated not by a desire to make video games for money but by a motivation to
make video games for his own family. Smith is the father of
three, and the experience of parenthood seems to have defined and completed his understanding of games. "We focus
on the reactions of children," he says. "Specifically my two
boys." For Smith, making video games for a younger audi-

ence is clearly a personal matter. The ultimate judge and jury of his life's work will be his own children, and that means that games development is more than just a job.

Smith's joy was evident as he sat next to me, showing me what he had made. It was gaming that had allowed him to create something unique and given him a mission. And his purpose wasn't some mysterious tier of administration or paperwork that would be alien and abstract from the lives of his children; instead, it was right here in front of us. We picked it up and we played.

## THE LABEL

The journalist Will Self once remarked that he would probably identify himself as a Londoner before identifying himself as a man, so important was the effect of the city on his psyche. In a similar way, I would probably identify myself as a gamer more than a writer, a human being, or a European citizen. The same is true for many other gamers: their job and ethnicity are subordinate to the fact of how their leisure time is spent. The classification "gamer" has become a badge of honor and, occasionally, a badge of shame. The label has (at least in the West) taken on a peculiar potency that doesn't quite seem parallel with "cinemaphile" or "art lover." Perhaps it's because gamers have been to some degree vilified and mocked that they have felt a need to grasp onto and highlight their identity. They have appropriated the term for their own uses.

The blogger Alice Taylor has mused on this subject a number of times in her endless trawl through the most obscure corners of gaming culture. "If everyone's a gamer, or even a majority, then 'gamer' will lose its tribal status," she told me. "It's currently a subculture, an identity statement. It will just become another ordinary 'doing' label: viewer, watcher, listener, gamer." Taylor's blog is largely motivated by her love of picking up on the gamer label: she blogs fashion and furniture, phones and furry toys, each item emblazoned with or inspired by the iconography and language of gaming. Gamers like Taylor are endlessly absorbed in the active process of bonding themselves with these symbols, the icons of their enjoyment. The tattoos stained into the skin of a number of my friends testify to the visceral reality of their commitment to these gaming identities.

Of course, the gamer label only identifies an indefinite aspect of a person. We don't all play the same games or even place the same value in games. Nevertheless, there does seem to be a difference between those people for whom games are little more than a distraction and those for whom games are of defining importance. Gamers have been changed in some of the ways I have already listed here but also in many other ways besides. It's possible that the gamer label to some degree matches up with the industry's internal identification of "hard-core" and "casual" gamers. This distinction has proven to be something of a myth but has nevertheless been used by developers and publishers to distinguish between the kinds of people who will simply dabble in the odd game of *Solitaire* or freeware *Mah-jongg* and those who commit vast amounts of time and money to habitual gaming. The latter people, to my mind, are the true gamers.

The habitual, hard-core gamers are people who have discovered something essential in gaming. What these people get from video games cannot be found elsewhere, and it is difficult to determine precisely what that thing is (although I suspect it has something to do with their personal projects of staying entertained). The range of possible gaming experiences is so vast that any survey will rapidly be overwhelmed or lose its way: gaming is no longer readily described or bracketed. The local status of a Japanese arcade hero hammering his way through epically difficult fighting games on a single credit seems worlds apart from the solitary hours I spent locked into the epic ultradetailed private fantasy world of the *Elder Scrolls* game *Oblivion.* What my retro-loving friend gets from the ancient classics of *Yar's Revenge* and *Breakout* seems to have little connection with the drunken evenings of *Guitar Hero* we enjoy elsewhere. The experiences that video games provide, the services they offer, cover a vast spectrum of possibility. We use *Tetris* on our mobile phone to make a train journey pass quickly, we turn a *Final Fantasy* game into "duvet terrain" when we're feeling tired and emotional. For hard-core gamers, video games have done more than distract or entertain us. They're vital experiences in which we've uncovered something useful, something vital in our lives.

One of these hard-core gamers, an adopted Londoner, is Leo Tan. He is a man whom I first met with his face illuminated by the screen of a handheld Nintendo. Does he think of himself primarily as a gamer? "Yes, completely," he says, "but I wouldn't say it has ever been a revelation at any point; I didn't wake up one day and think, 'Holy shit, I'm a gamer!' I suppose I'm just as likely to identify myself as Scottish, if it makes someone more comfortable."

Given Tan's personal history, it seems strange that he should worry about whether the gamer label would make people feel uncomfortable. He's right, though: the unfamiliar often does make people nervous. Tan knows all about that. He grew up on the Pennyburn, a council estate on the outskirts of Kilwinning, a small town in the west of Scotland. It was a place where "the schools have bars on the windows and huge fences to keep the children in, and all the mental kids carry Stanley blades."

Tan's memories of that time are grim. "Growing up there

was not much fun for me, who felt like the only Chinese kid within a thousand miles. Loads of fighting and being beaten up by huge Scots, a general fear of being out on the streets." For him, as for thousands of other children, games allowed a route for escape, a tunnel out of a place where there was no option to belong. It was the perfect alternative to ugly reality and to looming boredom: "Gaming was my escape when going out on the streets was no longer valid. Life at home was hell thanks to an alcoholic mum and an abusive step dad. My life consisted of getting out of the house whenever they were at home or staying in my room playing games whenever they were out at the pub. Much of my time out of the house was spent at a friend's playing games. Whenever I look back on my childhood, I can mostly remember just the games. Nostalgia for some people is remembering fields and playing soldiers in the trees; for me, it's *Roland on the Ropes* on the Amstrad CPC 464 and *Captive* on the Atari ST. Those worlds and my time in them provide the basis for all of my reminiscing." Tan is not alone in these memories.

When he grew up, Tan did something that probably doesn't come naturally to all kids who have spent most of their youth savoring computer games: he became a hairdresser. But even with this new career of haircuts and expensive shampoo, the computerized pastimes were not forgotten; Tan still bought and played everything he could. More important, though, he continued to find friends who had the same interests, people with the same ideas about games. He found much of this companionship on Internet game forums, such as the one hosted by the infamous British video game magazine *Edge:* "I was on it at least a few hours a day, which seems like a tremendous waste of time in hindsight. Or at least it would if it hadn't have got me my job. On the forum, I met [London-based public relations executive] Simon Byron, my current boss. I was getting bored with hairdressing, so after ten years of talking to hot girls about their sex lives, I asked Simon Byron for a job. Literally, I said, 'Can I have a job?' and he said, 'Yes.' That was it, really. I didn't really have a job interview or anything. I joined the games industry solely on my forum posting. Simon thought I could write and that I knew about games, and that was enough."

Echoing the sentiments I've heard from dozens of other gamers over the years, Tan recalled how he suddenly felt at home in a job where he got to talk about and work on the things he loved: "I've spent a lifetime feeling separated from everything and everyone around me. Things that I've cared about have not, by and large, been the things that other people around me care about. I have made some incredible friends growing up who also love games, but by and large we were not part of the 'community,' for lack of a better term." The video games that gave the young Tan something to escape into had ended up giving a focus to his adult life, just as it had done for me, Smith, Wedgwood, and countless other Londoners. Tan, however, had gone one better than any of us.

When working on the marketing for the rhythm-action masterpiece *Guitar Hero,* Tan and his colleagues arranged a publicity stunt at Donnington rock festival, the United Kingdom's largest heavy metal event: they would play *Guitar Hero* on stage in the opening hours of the concert. In a life that had been framed by gaming, this seemed like the ultimate achievement, a ludicrous, triumphant epiphany of video gaming.

Tan swells with pride at the mere mention of the event: "We opened for Guns 'N' Roses," he boasts. "Technically speaking, we opened for everyone. Gibson gave us their stage, so we just plugged in and went for it. We were really scared. We had no idea what the crowd would do when they saw our plastic guitars. We thought the worst that can happen would be bottles of piss thrown at us or maybe the crowd rushing the stage and smashing our faces in, so when we opened, my hands were shaking and I missed easy notes. Our tent quickly filled, as we were the only music anywhere, and they loved it. I think most of the crowd knew the game. They were cheering for songs during the options screen, and we had kids up on stage playing. Most of them were nailing the final tier songs on *Expert;* some played behind their head. It was incredible. It was the exact opposite of our worst fears. And playing *Guitar Hero* on stage is a completely different experience to playing at home. At home, you might feel like a guitar god; but on stage, people are screaming, and when you come off, they swamp to the sides to try to talk to you. It's exhilarating in a way that I'll never experience elsewhere. And it was a game. *And everyone knew it was a game."* Somehow, impossibly, Tan had been there when gaming turned into rock and roll. How's that for entertainment?

◄ SEOUL ►

# A Gamers' World

## OUTLANDISH THINGS

Travel in the video game industry means intercontinental city hopping. There are one or two games that were created out in the wilderness (such as the sheep farm where the techno-hippie Jeff Minter developed *SpaceGiraffe*), but their numbers are few and their budgets low. Bringing together high-technology communications and large teams of people means that games are generally made in built-up areas. These teams require the infrastructure and the managed office space that modern cities provide. Consequently, I have seen more than my fair share of downtown IT business districts—in Seattle and Dallas; Washington, D.C.; Los Angeles and San Francisco. I've visited endless corporate offices, usually to sit in a spare room and escape for a few hours to a fantasy realm: occult World War II, a 1930s gang war, postapocalyptic Eastern Europe, the fleshy surface of distant planets. This is the job, and while the venue is almost always somewhere with an air-conditioned office, I never know where games will take me. In March 2005, however, I did have a choice about where I would end up, and it took me to Seoul, South Korea.

Early March in Korea was a gloomy sight, and the drive from the airport provided a gradual introduction to the city's ramshackle immensity. The road hugged a smoggy coastline, heavy with industry and desolate-looking fishermen. Vast cargo craft sat out at sea, ready to depart with billion-ton shipments of hatchbacks, plastic rabbits, or shoes. The airport route was littered with leftover moments of cold war paranoia: our coach passed hilltop antiaircraft missiles, sinister in their battlefield camouflage.

Rounding a bend in the coast, we saw the giant conurbation rising up: the city is expansive and high-rise. The exploded population has been quartered in grim-looking apartment blocks that are often emblazoned with numbers. There seems to be little evidence of the older, pastoral world that Korea once belonged to, although it is still there, hidden in the backstreets and tourist cloisters. Everything that was flattened in the war was rebuilt long ago in concrete, freeways, and television antennae. Still, Korea's most intensive reconstruction in recent years has been virtual rather than physical. I had traveled to South Korea for much the same reason I had traveled to a dozen other cities across the world: to learn about video games. This was nevertheless a unique mission. I had come to the southern, Westernized portion of the Hermit Kingdom because there was too much secondhand information and speculation circulating about what was going on in the Internet cafés of Seoul. Blogging legend had it that Koreans played games en masse and that their most talented gamers were revered just like top sports players or TV celebrities are in Britain. The kind of geek stigma that existed in my world barely had a toehold out here. Provocatively, there were even reports of deaths, of obsessive gamers who played and played until their bodies simply gave out. There had even been rumors of amphetamines in the water supplies, keeping gamers un-

naturally wired for days at a time. I had heard so many outlandish things about Korean gamers that I needed to know
for sure whether they were true. And I had to know, most
important of all, what things were like for the gamers who
lived here.

South Korean gaming culture's most identifiably alien
gaming idiosyncrasy is that it is powered not by consoles
and handheld devices but by desktop computers. Unlike the
rest of the world, South Korea's gaming mainstream is not
based on Sony, Microsoft, and Nintendo products; it is powered instead by the humble, generic beige box. While the
PC has faded into the commercial background in Europe
and the United States, it is the major platform in South Korea. One even more radical feature of gaming culture in
Korea is the fact that the most popular games are usually
Korean products: Western games have had only limited impact on the South Korean gaming bubble. These commercial anomalies are intriguing in and of themselves, but
when you combine them with the astoundingly high number of Koreans who are playing games online—an estimated
5 percent of the total population regularly play online
games as compared to just 1.4 percent in Europe—then it
becomes clear that something quite unusual is afoot.

As my ride from the airport entered the central districts
of the vast, temperate metropolis, evidence of Seoul's many
gamers emerged. Huge advertising billboards featuring Korean games—*Archlord, Lineage II,* and *RF Online*—loomed
overhead. Towering names in English were subtitled with
Korean-language feature lists. These games have only recently been released in the West, and they met with an out-
standing lack of enthusiasm. To Western tastes, they
seemed not only ludicrously dull but often also bizarrely impenetrable. Most Korean games used the familiar *EverQuest*
formula of online level-based goblin-slaying role playing but

boiled it down to the bare bones. They boasted most of the features of Western games but were also comparatively dull, with massive groups of players killing massive groups of monsters or massive groups of other players, for massive amounts of points and gold. The Korean online role-playing games took elements of games that Western gamers found tedious—such as killing endless swathes of beasts to progress levels—and reduced them to their bare essence. A fraction of Westerners seemed to derive satisfaction from this kind of gaming, but it couldn't be the games that were to blame. The reason wasn't so much the games as the way we had learned to play and where.

South Korea's native gaming culture, which is fast becoming the model for most of East Asia, has always been markedly unlike its Western counterpart. Television makes the difference starkly apparent. Flick to a gaming channel and behold the spectacle as I did—many times. To a fanfare of Asian nu metal and the sound of a thousand screaming fans, a young Korean man entered a dazzling arena. Like an American wrestler at the heart of a glitter-glazed Royal Rumble, he strode down a ramp toward the stage. Adorned in what appeared to be a space suit and a large white cape, he stepped out to meet his opponent on the stadium's ziggurat focus. Amid a blaze of flashbulbs and indoor fireworks, he clambered up the steps, to be exalted by the thronging crowd. Only 20 years old and with no less than half a dozen TV cameras tracking his progress, this bizarre figure seemed to be unfazed by his predicament. Diligently he waved to the crowd.

At this point, my interpreter, the amiable Mr. Yang, leaned forward. "To my brother he is a great hero. My brother can't get enough of this. He has been to see him play many times." "So this guy has a lot of fans?" I said, knowing the answer but nevertheless incredulous. "Hundreds of thousands in his fan club," replied Yang. "Impossible to track the number of people who watch him play." This was impossible in part because the man on the stage was on Korean television almost every day. He was about to sit down and play what is close to becoming Korea's national sport: *StarCraft*. The man's name was Lee Yunyeol, or, in game, [RED]NaDa Terran. He was The Champion. In 2004 his reported earnings were around $200,000. He played the then six-year-old real-time strategy game for fame and fortune, and to many Koreans, he and his colleagues are idols.

Every night, over half a million Koreans log on to BattleNet and make war in space, many of them with dreams of becoming like Yunyeol. But NaDa Terran's skill is almost supernatural—running at a rate of several on-screen actions per second. Few people who play all day long will be able to claim a fraction of his split-second timing and pitiless concentration. Practicing eight hours a day, Yunyeol's methods and tactics are peerless. Well, almost peerless. In fact, two or three other players are able to command similar salaries. They might not have held the crown at the precise moment I was in Korea, but they would soon. At that moment, though, Yunyeol was king.

South Korea has five dedicated gaming channels, compared to none in the United Kingdom. While U.S. and European networks have made attempts to create shows about games since the early 1990s, none of them (except perhaps the bizarre youth game show *GamesMaster*) have really captured the popular imagination. American TV programmers seem sure that games are the future of television, but the ratings say otherwise. In the United Kingdom, late-night review shows or the odd bout of industry news is about the best we get, and game-related TV stunts have been mostly forgettable. A U.K. television show recently used the epic strategy title *Rome: Total War* to illustrate its series of historical battle reenactments, but little was made of the show's video game origins. Meanwhile, in Korea the aspirations of youth are mediated by video games and manifested through talk shows, games shows, and live broadcasts of gaming events. I took a few minutes to watch a show that pitted young gaming couples (who had met through playing *Lineage II*) against each other in a virtual battle arena. The smiling young Koreans commanded their sword-toting magicians with enviable proficiency. Their real faces were reduced to a corner of the screen as a commentator made the most of the blazing sword-and-sorcery action. Arcane energies fizzed, and the elegant game characters pirouetted in mimed death throes as the victors scored their killing blows. The winning couple were rewarded with a holiday to a very real beach somewhere in Thailand, and the pair cooed with delight as their spoils were revealed. The screen then returned to the studio, where a pop band waited to discuss their favorite video games with the bubbly silver-wigged presenter. It went on like this all day, every day. I flicked to another channel and watched intense young men controlling armies of tiny video game robots: the sport commentator's babble in the background was reaching a fever pitch. The pundits were amazed by the way a squadron of aliens circled a small blue valley. I jotted it all down as fast as I could in my spiral-bound notebook.

Out on the streets, there were even more palpable signs of gaming's hold on Korean culture. Thousands of Internet cafés are scattered throughout the city, and almost all of them are dedicated to gaming. When I wandered into a few of them in the early morning, I discovered exhausted-looking gamers already plugging away at mythic-looking dragons or swarms of flying eyeballs. I wanted to sit down and play, but I knew that few of the games supported an English option. This was where Korea's gaming culture was being defined—in social venues, such as bars that sold caffeinated soda, posters, and lots of gaming time to their hordes of customers. While Western gamers stay at home to play on their expensive Japanese consoles, the Koreans go out in search of a seat in a "PC Baang," one of their dedicated PC gaming cafés. A rented PC, a game of multiplayer kart racing, and perhaps a sly cigarette in the smoking section—these were the main ingredients for a typical evening. The combination has inspired a vibrant, youthful culture, where people go gaming to meet potential partners and where popular baangs have double-PC "love seats," allowing partners to sit close and play side by side, brushing fingertips as they reach for the conveniently placed drink holder.

Some of the baangs were gloomy and intimidating, while others were bright and spacious places. They reminded me of bars back in London, each one with its particular personality and species of clientele. In the late evenings, they were crowded with thronging Korean youth. Far from carrying any social stigma, video games had become the crux of an Internet-savvy, technologically enabled Korean entertainment culture. If the Koreans wanted to escape from the looming cellular apartment blocks, the uniformly silver sedans, and the gray, gray coastline, then they had found the ideal place—colorful, social, affordable, and filled with play. It was as if the roles of our bar culture and our Internet cafés had somehow been reversed and exploded. I wished, for an adolescent moment, that I belonged there.

In fact, as an adult living in Europe's alcohol-fueled nightlife, I often wonder about how different it must be to socialize in Seoul, where there seems to be no real drinking culture and few bars. What kind of radical cultural shift would be needed to bring that about in the West? Could games ever replace our traditions of getting horribly drunk and stumbling in the gutter? Nursing a mild hangover and recalling Friday night's transgressions makes me wish, at least temporarily, that they could.

## CAFÉ KOREA

How had this unusual culture come about? In this modern age of global homogeneity, at a time when Japanese game consoles and American software developers seem to have shaped everything we know about gaming, how did such an independent culture emerge? The answer is partly political and partly financial. Most of the major innovations in Western gaming culture have come from Japan. Its arcade games and wave after wave of home gaming systems have defined what it is to be a Western gamer at the start of the twenty-first century. American and European consumers, as well as game designers and publishers, have embraced the Japanese way of doing things; and the personal computer, although a steady force in gaming, has taken a backseat to home consoles and arcade machines. This has not been the case in South Korea. Thanks to a long-standing rivalry between the Korean Peninsula and its Japanese neighbor and to long memories of acts perpetrated during World War II, Japanese imports into South Korea are heavily taxed. This meant that Game Boys and PlayStations were exceptionally expensive during the 1980s and 1990s, the period when those same devices were selling so well in the West. Korean gamers had to rely on something cheaper and more readily accessible: the generic IBM PC.

Korea's commitment to the PC was also influenced by the networking potential of the average computer. While early consoles were solitary devices, unable to communicate or share information, PCs have long been able to hook up to larger networks. One of the most popular games in Korea, even to this day, is the 1998 sci-fi strategy game *Star-Craft*. This was the game I had seen treated like a spectator sport on Korean TV—a top-down map-based sci-fi battle game, where bases are built and scenarios won or lost in just minutes. Like many other PC games, *StarCraft* allows players to connect to other computers and play competitive games, either over a local network or over the Internet. This capacity for networked play helped to make *StarCraft* a surprise hit in Korea. Thousands of gamers got hooked by playing other Koreans—including the people they would meet out in the town.

When the first gaming cafés appeared, they featured rows of linked computers, each of them installed with games like *StarCraft*. Blizzard, the American company who produced the game, could not have predicted this niche appeal, and its popularity has not been matched anywhere else in the world. In contrast to Western youth, who were relatively slow to seize the opportunity provided by networked gaming, Korean young people got it almost immediately and were soon whiling away their evenings in competitive play. Strategy titles were only moderately successful in the West, with first-person shooters initially being more popular among American and European online gamers. Meanwhile, games like *StarCraft* became akin to a national sport for the multitudinous gamers of South Korea. Hundreds of thousands of people were drawn to play them, and thanks to the cheap and widespread proliferation of gaming through the baangs, they didn't even have to own a computer.

Koreans' desire to play *StarCraft* was further facilitated by the Korean government. The foresighted, tech-savvy administration was quick to grasp the significance of the Internet, and they worked hard to ensure that all urban buildings could be connected to high-speed data networks. At the end of the 1990s, when much of the East Asian economy was depressed, South Koreans were searching for new ways to develop business: the combination of multiplayer gaming and cheap Internet connections provided them with the answer. Not only could you play the people sitting next to you, but it was also possible to play people right across Korea. The PC Baang had found its purpose, and the country's gaming culture matured. The Internet cafés of Korea (of which there are now somewhere in the region of 16,000 in the greater Seoul area) were filled with people enjoying video games. These games were fast becoming the dominant form of leisure and entertainment in the nation as a whole.

Korean games have been adapted to the specific requirements of their audience, and this means that the companies that make them have adapted, too. For example, the fact that the studios do not have to write stories and script intricate action sequences has enabled them to concentrate on turning out endless levels and expansions for the multiplayer titles. Their online games might be vast and heavily detailed, but the designs only need to follow a few simple models that have already been fleshed out by the American companies that developed *EverQuest* and *Ultima Online*. Koreans also seem to enjoy player-versus-player conflict far more than do Western audiences, and designing games to incorporate this kind of mass conflict has been critical to games such as *Lineage* and *Archlord*.

The kind of challenging development and design that enables contemporary Western and Japanese games to feature believable characters and sophisticated AI was, in other words, unnecessary for the Korean model: real people filled the important roles, and the monsters fought by the players of massively multiplayer online games (MMOs) could be the simplest of automatons. Several of the Korean gamers I met in Seoul did, nevertheless, voice their dislike of native Korean games. One of them, a young Web journalist who wore Western gaming T-shirts, even described Korean gamers as "cursed." All the while showing me pictures of his attractive girlfriend, he explained that because the local media was so narrowly focused on the Korean way of gaming, very few Korean gamers had any idea of the wealth of experiences to be had in American and Japanese games. As a journalist and a hard-core gamer, my contact was familiar with games from across the world, but the majority of Korean consumers, he lamented, were not. He wasn't alone in his taste for more sophisticated games, but he was feeling lonely. Korea, he argued, had been left out of the international circus of gaming. Because of the monopolistic market, practically everything that had been sold to his contemporaries had originated in Korea and in the Korean model. Only California-based Blizzard, with their *Star-Craft* and *Warcraft* games, had really broken through.

Thanks to clever marketing and their high profile in baangs, homegrown Korean games such as *Crazy Racing Kart Rider* and *Lineage* enjoyed massive success. These Korean games do indeed display a much lower level of technological sophistication than their Western counterparts, but that's not always to their detriment. Their crucial attribute is not their complexity but their suitability for more casual play. Korean games provide this, and they provide ways for gamers to spend money without having credit cards. Being able to pay for aspects of the game in cash, over the counter in a baang, has been essential for a South Korean game's success. Korean gamers don't usually wish to own games, only to play them. They create accounts that allow them to sit down and play their favorite games on PCs anywhere in the country. Some titles, such as *MapleStory* and *Kart Rider,* are entirely free to play but can be augmented and expanded by buying in-game items over the counter in your gaming café or online via a Web site. A few won buys your game character a new sword or a token for a marriage with another player, and you can access these things wherever a connected PC has the game installed. You simply sit down, log in, and play.

This is a model that is being copied in game systems across the world. Publishers entice the gamers in with free games and then encourage them to spend once they're already engrossed in playing the game. It's a concept that Sony is examining for the online service of their latest console, the PlayStation 3; and a number of Western games have already inveigled us with free samples, paid for by supplementary in-game costs. The free multiplayer platform game *MapleStory* has recently become Korea's big international hit, with tens of millions of accounts created for the supercute adventure game. Of course, the Koreans have been using this kind of virtual backdoor finance for years. Ingenuity, if not innovation, seems to be the lifeblood of Korean gaming.

SEOUL GAMERS

As I explored Seoul, I met its gamers. I had expected the Korean gamer stereotype to be a little different from the Western one, and in some ways it was. In Korea, gaming is usually seen as hip, and the techno-nerd caricature that still permeates Western gaming has less traction, although baangs are often seen as seedy—perhaps something to do with the predominantly young male clientele. In fact, I learned that just a few months before my trip, there had been a demonstration march in the city for gamers wanting to "clean up" the baangs. If these outlets were better regulated, the marchers argued, then gaming would become more of a family event. Making baangs cheerier and smoke-free was top of the agenda. It was as if the ubiquitous gaming world postulated by Alice Taylor (and which I described in "The Big Smoke") had already come to be: a place where the label "gamer" connotes "person seeking entertainment" more than anything else.

Some of Korea's young people nevertheless take gaming pretty seriously. They view it as more than a good time or a way to meet a partner: they're looking for fame and fortune, too. On a Friday night, in a cinema complex in Seoul's immense underground mall, the COEX, I attended a session of the regular live broadcast of the Ongamenet Starleague, one of Korea's major pro gaming leagues. After pausing briefly at a row of public *World of Warcraft* booths (where, of course, my European log-in didn't work), I headed underground to the oddly situated TV studio. The league was one of two cash-prize *StarCraft* competitions in which the top ten players in the country would compete for tens of thousands of dollars in prize money. At the front of the room, watched by a dozen cameras and several hundred pairs of eyes, two *StarCraft* players battled it out. The techniques of both players had been refined over hundreds—even thousands—of hours of play, but it was clear that the handsome, logo-emblazoned pro was soon going to vanquish his beleaguered, perspiring, amateur opponent.

I imagined how intoxicating it must have been to play games so competitively and so publicly. My experience of competition told me that the sheer act of gaming was thrilling enough to be endlessly compulsive, but when you factor in the lure of large amounts of money and the rows of young women who sit intently watching the games, it was not difficult to see why young Korean men dedicated themselves so completely to this eight-year-old strategy game. The top half-dozen Korean *StarCraft* players were on national TV every day, and memberships in their fan clubs ran into the hundreds of thousands. These young gamers had made thousands of dollars from sponsorship and prize money, and their careers were only occasionally interrupted by Korean military service. It was an enviable life, one that few Western professional gamers will ever know.

Western pro gaming has also been going on for years, but its focus and audience are quite different. First-person shooters are the most significant games in European and American pro gaming spheres, and the majority of the action has remained with a steadfast hard-core niche who have a limited public following. Regular events around the world have spawned a series of minor gaming celebrities, including the well-publicized Jonathan "Fatal1ty" Wendell, who trains constantly to play games and relies on big sponsorship deals to pay the bills. But Western pro gaming nevertheless remains distant from mainstream pop culture. It's hard to imagine it ever breaking into our TV schedules and our mainstream teenage obsessions, as it has done in Korea. The majority of Western gamers barely know of the existence of the pro gaming stars, much less watch them on TV. In contrast, the weekly newspapers I picked up from magazine stands in Korea were covered with photos of gaming stars smiling, talking, and accepting large signed checks.

Away from the corner, on one side of the room, I stood next to the Starleague TV producer, In Ho Yoon. We watched as the Zerg attack on the Terran base raised a cheer from the crowd. Ho Yoon quietly explained how TV had turned *StarCraft* into a self-perpetuating phenomenon. The very fact that it had started to show up on the TV shows organized by obsessed gamers meant that sponsors had become interested. Once there was money involved, more people had started to play, and the competition, in turn, became more demanding. The escalating numbers of

*StarCraft* enthusiasts also increased, encouraging larger sponsors to offer greater amounts of money. Now the game has at least half a million people playing online each night, and two of the five gaming TV channels feature obsessively dissected reruns of important games, day in, day out. Earlier in the week, I had watched the end-of-season championship on a tiny TV in the corner of a game developer's office—the televised event took place in an indoor arena similar to a basketball stadium. Fireworks and thousands of screaming fans greeted the *StarCraft* masters as they ascended the stage to take to their keyboards and sponsored mice. Ho Yoon told me that people would camp outside the stadium for 24 hours before the event, just to get the best seats. I thought he might be joking. He wasn't.

Later that evening, I attended the launch of a new game, *Guild Wars*. I sat at a large table with dozens of Korean game industry people and watched as pop stars and television hosts joked and jostled for the limelight. A "comedy" celebrity match served as a warm-up for the main event, in which the best Korean teams, who had been testing the game for months prior to the launch, would duke it out for a check worth tens of thousands of Korean won. One of the people sitting at the table with me tried to come up with Western celebrity equivalents for those unrecognizable Koreans on the stage. "You know Chris Evans?" he asked, to my enormous incredulity. "This man is the same." My companion pointed at a guffawing TV presenter with glasses and dyed blonde hair. He was comparing him with Britain's own off-the-rails megapopulist former TV mogul. (Evans, for the uninitiated, was the biggest thing on U.K. TV for about ten years—his endless cheer and zany concepts allegedly made TV "fun" again. He enjoyed massive fame and wealth before marrying a teenage pop star and crashing into drink-related scandal and obscurity.)

Later on in the proceedings, my companion produced a Sony PSP, the handheld console that had just been released and had found its way onto Korean shelves in rather limited quantities. I silently thundered through the perfectly realized, miniaturized highways of *Ridge Racer,* while the wizards and monks on the screens above me became embroiled in magical combat. The audience gazed upward, watching the fantasy conflict while they digested their booze and dinner. I gazed downward and raced into a caricatured Tokyo.

Perhaps it was the champagne fused with jet lag or the fact that I was on the top floor of a seemingly infinite shopping mall, but I felt as though I had stepped through a bubble. I was exhausted and nauseous. I caught a glimpse of my eyes in a mirror and saw raw red where the whites should have been. Too many screens, not enough sleep. I slipped out and got a cab back to the hotel.

## SIGNIFICANT TV

For years now, I had noticed that some of the distinctive features of Korea's gaming culture were emerging, albeit tentatively, in my own backyard. My conversation with Ho Yoon about the self-perpetuating relationship between *Star-Craft* and television echoed another conversation that I had had a couple of years before with the creators of the bombastic American multiplayer shooter *Unreal Tournament.* One of their business masterminds, Jay Wilbur, postulated that broadcast television tournaments would be required for their game to really hit "the mainstream." If anyone with a gamepad or a keyboard had a chance of making money or just being on TV, Wilbur reasoned, the audience would explode. All their North Carolina studio had to do, he supposed, was to make a good enough game. But this prediction has not yet panned out: to this day, games have no significant TV presence in the West, and I think that this fact has little to do with the quality of the games themselves. *Unreal Tournament* has been consistently amazing, but it is possible that this kind of gaming simply isn't suited to TV viewing. Or maybe it's the audience themselves.

Korea's televised obsession, *StarCraft,* is highly polished, but it's hardly an example of the best that modern gaming has to offer. It's a traditionalist base-building, resource-gathering top-down strategy game, of which there are dozens of examples. These games are meticulous, high-speed battles involving a large map and dozens of invented units. It demands continuous concentration over manufacturing and combat, with players making hundreds of decisions each minute. The tiny marines and crude aliens are tremendously ugly by contemporary standards, and the game has been surpassed in any number of areas by modern multiplayer strategies. It's old, and it's definitely not sexy. The most up-to-date versions of *Unreal Tournament* are, by contrast, feats of futuristic technology, with incredible visuals and faultless construction. Considering this, it seems unlikely that the reason why games have never acquired a TV following in the West has much to do with game design. The kind of cultural environment that has allowed games to flourish in Korea does not exist in Europe or the United States, and it is precisely that cultural environment that has enabled Korea to have multiple gaming TV channels and to become a mecca for professional gaming across the globe.

The international finals of the World Cyber Games (a gaming event that now has regional stages in 20 countries) are regularly held in Seoul, and the Koreans dominate the strategic categories. First-person shooters like *Quake* and

*Counter-Strike* are far less popular in Korea (partly because the average computer is less powerful and therefore unable to support these games and partly because of the lack of commercial presence by popular Western companies), so American and Scandinavian teams currently dominate these categories. These teams, usually consisting of young men between 18 and 25, are comprised of the most dedicated gamers the West has to offer. They play continuously in online leagues (topping the kind of competitions I used to dabble in as a *Quake* player) and regularly compete in sponsored competitions. Game publishers and hardware manufacturers tend to foot the bill, and lavish events are created for these teams of young men, to find out who is the most talented. These teams do not, however, have much of a following in their countries of origin. Westerners do not watch *Counter-Strike* on TV and are much more likely to be playing *Quake* than following the activities of its top professionals.

In 2005 I was briefly involved in setting up a professional gaming team in the United Kingdom, and one of my key concerns was whether or not the team would be able to automatically qualify for sponsorship to fly to Korea. Samsung, the sponsor at the time, would only provide flights for the top teams, and without a U.K. event and a winning team, we wouldn't be automatically eligible. Paying for five men to travel to the other side of the world was not going to be cheap, but if the team was to be taken seriously, it needed more than a sponsor and a bank of expensive PCs: it needed to be seen in South Korea. It was almost as if South Korea alone legitimized what we were trying to do. Certainly, few people in the United Kingdom seemed to care. Our choice of U.K. teams was between an older group, who were young professionals with a team manager, and some kids who were barely out of school. We

chose to give the money to the younger, spottier team—
plumping for the underdogs in a rather typically British
fashion. I couldn't help thinking that we would somehow be
reinforcing the stereotype of European games nerds when
those boys finally landed in Korea, but the joyous way that
they received the news of their sponsorship made me simply not care.

Despite all the excitement that pro gaming has generated among gamers in South Korea and the money it has
raised for pro teams in Europe and the United States, I am
nevertheless skeptical of its "professional" status. The
handsome young gaming pros of South Korea did not con-
vince me that sponsored professional gaming is where the
future of gaming lies. For over a decade, there have been
gamers and games companies trying to promote video gaming as a sporting spectacle, but the truth is that it remains
an awkward spectator sport. It's an interesting avenue of
possibility for a small clique of gamers, perhaps; but the
low number of people who watch video games played by the
pros outside Korea suggests that the most important aspect
of gaming is its interactivity. I've seldom been as bored as
I have been watching pro gaming tournaments, especially
when they're for a game I'm actually interested in playing.
For these reasons, I believe that Korea's televised Star-
leagues reflect a cultural singularity within Korea, not an
indication of where global gaming will go in the future. Perhaps as we globalize, the era of pro gaming will be lost altogether. Then again, given the sponsorship money raised,
maybe it will one day begin to self-perpetuate, as Wilbur
suggested.

Still, I don't believe that the future of games is in live
competition, on television or anywhere else. Fragments of
that future do nevertheless exist in Korea. I detected clues
in a slender and bashful young woman called Lee In Sook.

## SLENDER AND BASHFUL

Korea's youth live in a conservative, family-orientated society. They are generally polite and often shy. Games are not their only outlet for rebellion and self-expression—the frequent outlandish sight of leather-clad bikers with boom boxes built into their motorbikes attests to that—but they are a cheap and convenient way for gamers to sink their energies into something other than schooling, work, or their family. Without the same bar and dating culture as the West, Koreans have dabbled in inventing their own youth social scenes, of which baangs have been a part. Korea's youth culture is, in some sense, still an artifact of Westernization, but it is one driven by the quiet, inward-looking nature of the people of this quiet peninsula.

Lee In Sook seemed fairly typical of Korean youth. She was dressed casually but smartly, with hints of alternative fashion in the buttons on her bag and in the peculiar-looking fashion magazines she was carrying (featuring cover models with blue and green sculpted hair and plastic clothes). My meeting with In Sook was arranged by a games company, NCsoft—one of Korea's largest. I had asked to meet one of their most hard-core gamers, though I had only the vaguest idea what this request meant. I thought perhaps it might be one of the leaders of warring *Lineage II* tribes, such as the beleaguered owner of a burger bar who I had read about in a U.K. newspaper. He had claimed he could not reveal his true identity because it would risk his actual life, so great was his in-game power. Game-playing thugs, the article claimed, could make his life very difficult, since he didn't wield the supernatural power of his avatar in the real world. I imagined the hard-core Korean gamer being something like a nerdy mafioso: a wiry young man with an Atari T-shirt, a cigarette, and a punk attitude, obsessed with maintaining power in a world that I would never see. But I was greeted instead by a small, bespectacled girl in pink and denim.

In Sook was a nervous, smiley Korean student in her early twenties. She didn't seem to know why this scruffy journalist from the United Kingdom was asking her questions, but she indulged me nonetheless. We spoke through a translator, and I wondered whether my interest in her gaming prowess made any sense to her. Did she understand why I found it unusual? She seemed profoundly normal—like any girl I might meet on the street back home, with a canvas bag on her shoulder and plastic folder full of university course work under her arm. Like many young Korean women she had taken to the fantasy role-playing world of *Lineage II* quite easily and had rapidly become immersed in its massively multiplayer workings. She was in fact in a similar position to the one I had found myself in a few years earlier, as an experienced player helping novices to learn the game. She devoted many hours to her character and was one of the few people to have a *Lineage II* avatar whose experience level numbered in the seventies. At that time, this was no mean feat, since creating a character at that level required at least 2,000 hours of play (which, by my rudimentary calculations, means just under four hours a day for 17 months). Like me during my most intensive *Quake* days, In Sook was obsessed with her chosen game. She laughed that she didn't go out to baangs enough and would rather stay at home to play, where there were fewer distractions and she could concentrate on the game. In Sook was engrossed and committed just as I had been a couple of years earlier. Was this really just a hobby?

The word *hobby* has peculiar connotations, and for that reason, I try to avoid using it in relation to games. But in this case, I could not. A hobby is a highly personal activity.

It is something we indulge in, spend money on, and care about despite—and perhaps because of—its nonessential nature. It's the opposite of working for money. Yet the importance of hobbyist activities is easily overlooked, especially when hobbies create the kinds of community that we seem to crave. Like any other group of friends, formed for whatever reason, through whatever shared interest, In Sook's small cadre of gamers were set to go on holiday together that summer. Most of them lived in Seoul, but they wouldn't necessarily have found each other without the conduit of *Lineage*. In this way, games are creating new links, beyond those created by work, school, or local neighborhoods; and that alone makes them powerful and significant. These best of friends might simply have passed each other on the busy streets of downtown Seoul if it hadn't been for their shared gaming interests. And the same could easily have been true for thousands of gamers across Seoul. Perhaps they had met as spectators at the *StarCraft* league or in a café while they competed at *Kart Rider*. Thanks to games, In Sook's circle of friends had ended up talking, becoming close, and then making sure that they hung out at the same cafés to play at the same games. Online games create shared experiences that are unlike those we might have in the real world. This is a quality of the medium itself—players who might not excel in conversation might well feel confident in text chat. In Sook didn't look particularly imposing, but her dedication to *Lineage* meant that she carried a great deal of power and influence in the game world. This paralleled my own experiences in some way: I could never organize a sports team, but I rapidly became an overcompetitive dad when faced with playing *Quake*. Among In Sook's gaming companions, as with the *EVE Online* fans I would eventually meet up with in Iceland, gaming had created an entirely new community within a community. These were personal connections that might otherwise have been absent, here in the heart of this teeming Asian city.

The simple fact that so many people have been brought together because of hours spent at a screen and keyboard is fast becoming recognized as one of the most significant positive effects that games are having on society. A January 2006 article in *Time* magazine, written by Ta-Nehisi Paul Coates, described the author's struggle to get anything done when he was obsessed with the online game *World of Warcraft*. I disagreed somewhat with his analysis of the situation (there's a difference between the problematic effects of gaming and the difficulties of personal motivation), but he did make an interesting statement about what online games offer people like him—and perhaps it is true of the people of South Korea as well. "What I came to understand," says Coates, "was that [*World of Warcraft*] was not necessarily an escape, but a surrogate for a community that is harder and harder to find in the real world." Coates referred to that traditional genre of intimate, almost tribal community that modern life seems to have dissipated. But his article made me wonder if it was really the case that gamers had re-created that older-genre community or if they had instead produced something unprecedented and new. Coates thought gaming was a surrogate for lost "village"-level mentality, but the evidence for this is unclear. Online games are usually far more like teeming cosmopolitan cities than stable provincial communities: the mix of people is enormously diverse, and you often find yourself being ignored by passersby or even accosted with unsettling propositions. You aren't sure who to trust, and many gamers will depend on previous acquaintances or real-world friendships as the basis for in-game socializing. Gamers are able to form random partnerships with complete strangers to complete very immediate objectives—killing a monster, for example—in a way that contrasts utterly with village life, where sudden cooperation with strangers is both infrequent and unlikely.

Nevertheless, like safe, well-run cities, online games provide hubs where gamers can congregate, communicate, and connect. Discussion forums may generate some friendships, while the activity of the games themselves, perhaps especially the element of collaboration, may generate others. Online friendships might blossom into real-world relationships (as has happened for the countless couples who have married after meeting in online games), or they may stay as digital relationships. I personally have perhaps 40 or 50 gaming buddies whom I have never met and probably never will. There's no need to meet them—no reason for our real-world concerns to collide. Our relationship is about getting games working and enjoying them as a team. We discuss games and play them, and that's the limit of our interaction. Most of us don't need the bother of extra real-world commitments.

Online games are not replacing traditional forums for socializing and bonding; they are instead providing new reasons to interact and exchange ideas. They represent new possibilities for human communication. And part of the appeal is their flexibility. The relationships you forge only need to be taken as far as you want to take them—unlike in a village or any other "real-world" social venue. In Sook's gaming companions might have met and bonded to form a new network of real-world friends, but many more gamers will only indulge to play with other gamers online and will never choose to meet them or to take their interaction further. It is a matter of choice.

This, I thought, was why In Sook's circle of friends, rather than the fierce competition of the professional gamers, was where the important future of games lay.

Games stand to change not simply individual imaginations or personal finances but the possibilities for interaction and socialization across our different cultures. This is no grand cultural revolution: it is a subtle wave, a gradual tectonic shift in the way we live, which will only make its true effects known over the course of many years. Games are growing, spreading, changing; and like the proliferation of TV, mobile phones, or automobiles, it's a change that will have far-reaching effects that cannot be easily predicted or defined. Chasing headlines that read "Games Are the New Sport" or "Kids Who Play Games for a Living" makes a crude statement about what really matters within gaming. The important changes will come from those smaller ripples that change how millions of people live, think, and socialize on a daily basis, not just the hard-core niches.

## THE RISING SUN

It's impossible to say for certain whether Korea's kind of social café-culture gaming will spread to Europe and America, but at this point, it seems unlikely. And perhaps we Western gamers will never even feel its lack, since we'll have other gaming projects to hold our attention: a succession of dazzling manic shooters, artificially intelligent game characters that take us to dinner parties, or interactive genres of storytelling that far surpass Hollywood traditions—billion-dollar, seamless productions, costing us hundreds of dollars to play. It is also quite possible that Western stay-at-home-for-gaming tendencies could soon be a minority trend.

For now, North America remains the most heavily populated gaming market, but South Korea's neighbors, including megapopulous Indonesia and China, are rapidly accruing their own "PC Baang" culture and playing much the same kind of games as the Koreans. (There's even an MMO involving Indian mythology in development, with publishers recognizing that the subcontinent might not be far off this kind of gaming event horizon.) Chinese gamers, encouraged by new business possibilities in China's rapidly expanding cities, are setting up thousands of gaming cafés. Around 95 percent of all games played in China are played on desktop computers. South Korea could soon represent an early prototype of how video games will be played in the modern East Asian culture. Of course, it's possible that this well will run dry and that gaming in Asia will turn inward and become domesticated, as it has in Japan and America, where gaming arcades are increasingly rare. But it's arrogant to think that the Western model of video games as entertainment via expensive TV consoles is the only possible model. The way video games end up being used could be very different from how we currently imagine them, more like going to an exclusive casino or a bar than sitting in a shed, tinkering with tiny pixelated people. South Korea offers a glimpse of what such an extroverted video game future might be like.

Asia will of course find its own uses for Western products, too. The Western online gaming paragon *World of Warcraft* has approximately 3.5 million Chinese players at the time of this writing, and there will no doubt be many more by the time you read these words. The lovely Lee In Sook could one day represent millions of Asian gamers, for whom socialization through gaming is the norm.

In 2006 the creator of *The Sims,* Will Wright, observed that "computers have ended up being more about communication than computation." It's the ability to chat and obtain information via the Web that is most important to us, not the number-crunching power of our computer. If trends within Asia remain steady, then we might soon be able to say something similar about games: that they ended up being more about people socializing and playing together than about snazzy graphics or sophisticated gameplay mechanics.

What really matters here is not the visual complexity or the gameplay design of the games themselves but the form of the technology that enabled them to bring people together in the first place: massively multiplayer worlds plug thousands into the same communicative sphere and do not necessarily require powerful PCs. The idea of having fun in a colorful fantasy world might be the lure, but it is the interaction with other people that provides the hook. The specific game is almost incidental: *Lineage* and then *Lineage II* just happened to be the biggest MMOs in Korea at one time, and many similar products, such as *World of Warcraft*, now provide similar opportunities for people across the world. What mattered in Korea was not so much the model of the game world, the (often rather dismal) activities on offer, or even the experiences of large-scale combat that they sometimes afforded; it was the fact that it needed to be played as a team that had to communicate to succeed. Playing alone, as I discovered when I found *Quake III*, can only keep us occupied for so long. Games might be interesting, but they're seldom as interesting as people.

There were millions of gamers worldwide by the end of the 1990s, and their numbers are still growing. But gamers are now awash in new ways to communicate. Blogs, Web sites, and forums offer gamers spaces in which to discuss games and indulge their interests, while the online games themselves provide new ways to meet, argue, interact, fight, and play. They even offer entirely new reasons to get upset or angry. As East Asia rapidly becomes Internet-enabled and increasing numbers of new gamers are online, they are also finding ample cause for criticism and concern. Gamers bring their own tastes and opinions with them, and many of them demand games that reflect and reinforce their extragame lives. Like their neighbors in Korea, the Chinese are, for example, often keen to play games that are based on familiar, local themes. Adapted versions of foreign imports, such as *World of Warcraft,* are popular, but so are native games, like *Fantasy Westward Journey* (henceforth *FWJ*). NetEase, the huge and highly successful Chinese technology company that operates *FWJ,* has rapidly become one of the most popular—and most controversial—of Chinese online gaming companies. *FWJ* is popular partly because it only requires an Internet link and a low-spec PC to play it and partly because its theme (the eponymous westward journey) derives from classical Chinese myth and legend. At the moment, *FWJ* has around 25 million registered accounts, and up to 1.3 million people log on to play concurrently during any given evening. In the summer of 2006, the game was host to an unprecedented event in online gaming: a virtual protest involving up to 80,000 players.

The chain of events that led up to the in-game demonstration went something like this: On July 4, 2006, administrators of *FWJ* suspended a gamer with an anti-Japanese name. The gamer, who had already been playing for two years with the same moniker and who claimed to have spent around US$3000 on the game, refused to change his handle in order to comply with NetEase policies. The following day, NetEase dissolved one of the largest player alliances in the game, called The Alliance to Resist Japan. The company explained their actions by saying that they would not "permit any names that include those that attack, insult, or mislead with respect to race, nationality, national politics, national leaders, obscenity, vulgarity, libel, threat, religions, and religious figures" (www.zonaeuropa .com). This whole ordeal might all seem politically chaotic to a Western audience, but some Chinese players simply saw sinister motives at work. Outspoken *FWJ* gamers had begun to circulate rumors that Japanese commercial influences were going to change things within their game. It was said that Chinese national symbols were going to be replaced with pigs and that Japanese iconography was being covertly installed by the developers. Meanwhile, players were said to be unhappy that one of the buildings within the game world had been decorated with a painting reminiscent of Japan's symbol of the rising sun. NetEase denied that it was being bought out by Japanese business or that it intended to change any patriotic content. They argued that, on the contrary, these were valid, China-friendly decorations. The argument spread, and even otherwise apolitical gamers began to congregate to discuss the problematic aesthetics. By July 7, the situation had become critical, and players assembled inside the game to protest at what they saw as an injustice. They wanted NetEase to withdraw the policy, change the decor, and allow anti-Japanese sentiments to be freely expressed. The protest started out with something like 10,000 players and ended up with 80,000— more than 60,000 higher than the game's average population at the time. Exactly how many of those players were actually protesting and how many had come along simply to witness the spectacle is impossible to say. But it was nevertheless an unprecedentedly large event for any virtual world.

The *FWJ* event demonstrates just how much Chinese gamers valued their game. They were closely enough identified with it to be moved to demonstrate, in massive numbers, against a perceived infringement of their rights and beliefs. This suggests, of course, that gamers do not compartmentalize gaming or dismiss it as trivial fantasy removed from real life. On the contrary, the fantasy is so deeply significant that even apparently minor slights against Chinese patriotism provoked intense anger. To understand this anger, it's worth remembering that Japan and China, like Japan and Korea, have had a troubled history that is essentially unparalleled in Western politics. Japan is still seen as an aggressor, although now an economic aggressor rather than a military one. The modern, technologically enabled Chinese are no less politically driven than older generations, and the desire for independence from Japanese influence remains strong. This trend has been exacerbated by the Chinese government's efforts to use games to promote state-endorsed national culture. Gaming has been recognized as an official sport, and numerous government-sponsored companies in games development have begun to release dozens of "patriotic" games. This level of state investment can only have fueled the *FWJ* gamers' beliefs that their game should be brought in line with accepted patriotic sentiments.

MIT media academic Henry Jenkins, who studied the *FWJ* incident, concluded that "the Chinese government's efforts to regulate game playing—and to promote games as part of the national culture—have transformed what might have been a mere pastime into a more politically charged environment." What was most significant, Jenkins noted, was that this was an argument about how the game fitted into the wider culture. The demonstration was not about some change within the game or some issue of game play (like the perceived weakness of gnomes that led to minor protests in *World of Warcraft*); it was about national character and China's place in the world. Players and the games company were articulating the unique dilemma that has dogged online games in varying degrees over the past decade: namely, how to bridge the so-called client-server divide, by balancing the wishes of game creators, on the one hand, and players, on the other. NetEase had one view of how the game should be, and the gamers had another. But how a game ends up is often a mixture of the two. In this case, NetEase wanted it to be politically correct, while players had a quite different view of how it should reflect their own patriotism, and the parties only came to a settlement after a fair amount of disruption. Like other games that I will go on to talk about later in this book, *FWJ*'s game world had become an idea that was continually being contested and influenced both by its creators and its players. This contest is an important illustration of how games affect the people who play them.

## COMMERCIALLY FUELED

The *FWJ* incident may have dwarfed any other online protests, but it is far from the only example of games becoming entangled with real-world issues. In Europe and the United States, where games are often far less conformist than in Asia, there are numerous cases of gaming becoming embroiled in political conflict, although the reasons for these conflicts vary from game to game. Perhaps the most obvious and predictable instances of this involve censorship or content boundaries, such as when the game *San Andreas* came under scrutiny for having a previously undisclosed sex-based subgame hidden in the code. The revelation that it was possible to hack the game on both PC and console formats to reveal the abandoned minigame caused many politicians to call for new controls on games, and there was some controversy over whether the publisher, Take Two, had dodged what should probably have been an adult-only rating for the game. That the controversy stemmed from a barely accessible and nonexplicit sexual minigame rather than from the game's themes of casual ultraviolence or prostitution is cause for knowing smiles among many gamers. Missing the point has been typical of most of the moral panics that have engulfed video games. The gap between gamers and the people who are trying to regulate them is wide indeed. A quick trip to YouTube.com and a search for "*Daily Show*" and "video games" illustrate that point with satirical clarity.

Occasionally the issues that flare up within Western gaming resemble those that surfaced in *FWJ*, such as when Blizzard, the company that runs *World of Warcraft,* came under fire for outlawing explicitly gay and lesbian in-game associations (some "guilds" of the game world had intended to recruit specifically homosexual players). For Blizzard, it was a matter of maintaining the fiction and reducing the likelihood of harassment. For the members of the gay and lesbian guilds, however, this was a matter of freedom of expression. Just as in China, the issues of the real-world and fictional world were not sealed off from each other in the minds of gamers. This was not a film or a book, where the fiction was packaged and complete; the game was leaky, acted on, and generally subject to the desires of the players who paid to play it. Eventually Blizzard conceded that they should not impose such limitations on their players, but it's easy to see why they made such moves in the first place: the exact nature of the relationship between gamers, game world, and game creators has not yet been defined. The argument represents another instance of gamers feeling as if what happened in the game world was just as important as anything that might happen in day-to-day life. In cases like these, the wizened chestnut who suggests that "it's only a game" seems misinformed and out of touch.

The *FWJ* protestors thought that the alleged pro-Japanese imagery was corporate propaganda and that they were therefore being illegitimately influenced. Gamers seem particularly sensitive to the things that alter their gaming experience. They become so familiar with the game that even the slightest change can be detected. Usually our complaints are about some minor nuance of the way the game works—a slight change in physics parameters or the color of a hat—but the changes could equally be political.

Many gamers took exception to the gradual introduction of advertising into their game worlds. Recently, the online shooter *Battlefield 2142* became just one example of a game that had polarized opinion thanks to the inclusion of external advertising sold into its game environment. Reams of grumbling from gamers and fans of the series followed release, along with online guides on how to stop the ads appearing at all. This suggests that gamers (or at least some gamers) resent anything that unduly impinges on what they see as the pure experience of their game. Some play games precisely to get away from this kind of influence—whether political or commercial—while others revel in the indulgence of a particular belief. For the *FWJ* players, it was about the mythology of patriotic China, and for the players of a game like *America's Army* (a first-person shooter developed by the U.S. military), it is about celebrating their military culture.

Of course, there is an obvious corollary to this observation: if gamers are so sensitive to the messages their games convey, what better way to reach gamers than through their games? It seems clear that the more gamers there are and the more culturally significant games become, the more external forces will to want to use games to influence gamers. Gaming will soon be just another weapon in the arsenal of political propagandists.

# Propagandists

## PROPAGANDA DEVICE

One of the most widely discussed politicized games is called *America's Army*. The game is a marketing tool, commissioned by the U.S. Army to encourage interest in the military. The multiplayer, first-person shooter was a quasi-simulatory game of combat tactics, inspired by the popularity of militaristic games such as *Counter-Strike*. Having been paid for with U.S. tax dollars, it was made freely distributable over the Internet in 2002. Nothing unusual there, but there was something distinctly strange about the game itself: although it is played by two competing teams, the interface is designed such that you always play against "terrorists" and you always play as a marine. No matter which team you are on, it always appears to be the American team and therefore the "good guys." *America's Army* wore its politics on its sleeve.

The U.S. Army has openly admitted that *America's Army* is a propaganda device, intended to show the U.S. Army in a positive (and presumably entertaining) light. "In elementary school kids learn about the actions of the Continental

Army that won our freedoms under George Washington and the army's role in ending Hitler's oppression. Today they need to know that the army is engaged around the world to defeat terrorist forces bent on the destruction of America and our freedoms," says the game's Web site. The same Web site is also integrated with links to military recruitment sites.

Some commentators have contended that the game's recruitment efforts involve far more than simply littering its FAQs with banner advertising. It has been alleged that the military actively collect statistics from the gamers who spend time in the game. Gary Webb, writing in June 2005 for the *Sacramento News and Review,* claimed that army recruiters were able to access information about players: "*America's Army* isn't merely a game, recruiting device, or a public relations tool, though it is certainly all of those things. It's also a military aptitude tester. And it was designed that way from the start." Webb believed the game was being used to train and identify possible soldiers.

I spoke to some of the players of another online team-based combat game, *Counter-Strike,* in my hometown. Aged between 15 and 18, they were mostly the children of wealthy families—privileged boys who liked to hang out at a local gaming center and perfect their skills. A few of them had played *America's Army* but had concluded that it was "lame" or simply laughable. It might have been free, but then so were a dozen other, better games. Like me, they saw little connection between the abstract processes of sitting in front of a computer screen watching for a flicker of distant khaki pixels, on the one hand, and picking up a real-life M16 to gun down the enemies of freedom, on the other. Had any of these kids ever even fired a real gun? Nope—they live in suburban England. Most of them had never even seen a genuine firearm.

Games do not prepare us for war. Even if our visual processing has been massively enhanced by years of *Robotron,* the brute reality of lugging heavy gear across vast tracts of desert or flying helicopters into a barrage of machine-gun fire remains a long way off. The intentions of the military to use games as recruitment tools seem outlandish, even misguided. Do any of us really confuse the things learned from games with the nightmare realities of a battlefield? Apparently some senior military officials think so. The director of the technology division at Quantico Marine Corps Base told the *Washington Post* in February 2005 that gamers—and hence some of today's army recruits—"probably feel less inhibited, down in their primal level, pointing their weapons at somebody."

To see that this is nonsense, get to know the kind of hard-core gamers who have ended up playing *America's Army* (the less astute gamer would never even know that this game existed). These are not new tech-savvy supertroopers; they are adjusted, often mildly cynical young men who know a lot about the Internet. Their future is most likely in computing or technology. Of course, the army has always wanted intelligent young men—it needs them. But if gamers genuinely are "less inhibited," then they certainly aren't any better prepared for facing actual combat. The book *Generation Kill* by Evan Wright attests to this fact. Wright, who rode with the elite First Recon unit in Iraq, describes how the soldiers discovered the true depths of their innocence as they shot real people. He describes how the men broke down when they saw the consequences of gunfire, and he speaks with frightening clarity of how there was no way that gaming, no matter how violent, could ever have prepared them for those experiences. These soldiers might have killed thousands on their PlayStations, but death up close was a completely different and unbearable experience, well beyond their coping mechanisms. Simulated death is not death.

Leaving aside such mercifully extreme cases, let's look at the propaganda uses of gaming in more detail. Many gamers are surprised to learn just how far the games-as-political-tool project has come in the past few years. Games now address a vibrant spectrum of issues, and there have already been a number of games that illustrate and discuss real-world problems, from suicide bombing to cancer. These are games that, rather than provide a merely entertaining escape portal, want us to look back at the world with fresh eyes when we log off. At the other end of the spectrum from *America's Army* is the development company Persuasive Games, whose games are compelling attempts at social and political satire. One of their games directly attacks working practices at Kinko's by allowing gamers to play with work-dodging employees, while another (the hilarious *Airport Insecurity*) makes a playful satire of the current overzealous security practices at international airports. As their creators admit, these are games with an agenda, and gamers, it seems, are now being targeted for agendas of all kinds.

Underpinning this trend is the recognition that games manipulate the people who play them in some interesting new ways. Being able to handle something, to interact with an idea rather than simply hear about it, is a potent effect. We enjoy playing games, even the most simplified ones, more than we enjoy reading blurbs or listening to lectures. The Nobel Foundation, set up to award international achievements in art and science, uses video games to explain the many startling accomplishments of its prizewinners. From DNA to *Lord of the Flies,* Nobel Foundation has a game to teach you about commendable human achievement (visit www.nobelprize.org).

The members of such venerable institutions aren't the only people that have realized games can be used to persuade their target audiences of what they believe to be truth. Militant gamers in Australia intended to make a political statement with the now infamous *Half-Life* modification *Escape from Woomera*. The amateur project highlighted the plight of those imprisoned in Australia's tough immigrant program. The developers explained: "With a first-person, 3-D adventure game, we invite gamers to assume the character of and 'live' through the experiences of a modern-day refugee. The effective media lockout from immigration detention centers has meant that the whole truth about what goes on behind the razor wire at Woomera, Baxter, Port Hedland, Maribyrnong, and Villawood remains largely a mystery to the Australian public. We want to challenge this by offering the world a glimpse—more than that even: an interactive, immersive experience—of life within the most secretive and controversial places on the Australian political and geographical landscape. In this way, *Escape from Woomera* will be an engine for mobilizing experiences and situations otherwise inaccessible to a nation of disempowered onlookers. It will provide both a portal and a tool kit for reworking and engaging with what is otherwise an entirely mediated current affair."

The Australian government was so upset by the publicity generated by this otherwise obscure game modification that the foreign minister at the time openly attacked it, publicly expressing his indignation and disgust. Of course, what was most significant about the project wasn't the controversy (although a bit of publicity always goes down well) but the way in which it illustrated the ability of games to teach people about difficult and unfamiliar subjects. Learning about the living conditions of immigrants and asylum seekers in a system that was recognizably cruel made for a powerful and politicizing experience. No wonder unhappy voices were raised in the Australian halls of power.

But there's more to this than upsetting the status quo. *Escape from Woomera* was, in its small way, teaching us how to lead a better, more ethical life. This game wasn't designed to improve hand-eye coordination or organizational skills; it was to improve souls. Just as works of literature have been celebrated for enlarging our capacity to feel empathy with and solidarity for many different kinds of people, so this particular game was encouraging us to identify with people whom we might not otherwise consider or know. By expanding our imaginative capacities in this way, games like *Escape from Woomera* seek to change the world.

Of course, there are plenty of examples that can easily be used to support a quite different—and much less encouraging—argument. The in-game slaughter of the attendees of a funeral held for a deceased *World of Warcraft* player presented a case of quite spectacular insensitivity. It revealed a significant swathe of gamers who radically failed to sympathize with their fellow gamers, treating them as little more than moving targets and ignoring the real-life tragedy they were trampling on. Perhaps, however, they were simply acting within the narrative conventions that the game delivered to them. Their game belonged firmly within the genre of bad guys versus good, and they played the bad guys. Had it been a game about tragedy and human loss, the gamers' responses and actions might have taken on quite a different character.

I've often discussed the odd phenomenon of "online sociopathy" with other games journalists. We've idly speculated that just as people display different degrees of sociopathy in their interactions with people in the everyday world, so gamers display different degrees of sociopathy in their interactions with game characters, whether human or

AI driven. Some gamers detect (and deliver) remarkably subtle nuances of meaning through game characters, while others will act like maddening infants, smashing, insulting, and destroying as if there were no other human observer present. Those who act the most moronic in games will often be entirely amiable folks when met face-to-face and only display these destructive traits in a video game world. The issue could be partly socialization: that they've never been taught how to play nicely in these particular environments. Or it could be psychological: an acute lack of game world empathy, a kind of cybersociopathy. I expect more nuanced understandings of gamer psychologies when researchers begin to study how people experience and behave in their "extended identity." The way that the *Fantasy Westward Journey* protesters (which I discussed in "A Gamers' World") reacted or the way that some people feel licensed to misbehave because "it's just a game" will all become part of a diverse and complex array of gamer profiles.

## SERIOUS GAMING

Mainstream games have not typically managed to convey emotional subtleties. The jury is out on whether it's even possible for games to convey much outside fear, excitement, and bewilderment. Many gamers do report episodes of sadness—most famously at the death of a *Final Fantasy* character, Aeris—or of joy at their achievements. But whether the tonal shades of experiential gray enabled by literature and film are possible in gaming is uncertain. I think one of the reasons that people have found online games such as *World of Warcraft* so compelling is that they are able to recognize the powerful human intelligence underpinning its avatars and Netspeak. Even distanced as we are, there's a good deal of possibility for emotional entanglement, in a way that there is not with computer-generated characters. Creating a "Turing Test" character—one that we cannot tell from a human being—is and will remain one of the great challenges of game design. We're seeing some big leaps forward, as anyone who has played *Half-Life 2* and seen its characters in motion will attest, but believable digital autonoma are nevertheless a long way off.

I want to focus on what games can and do deliver right now. Identifying what games do best is a first step toward applying games to meet specific purposes, purposes other than entertainment alone. Some gamers have attempted to do precisely this by producing games that are intended to edify more than entertain. The Serious Games Initiative (www.seriousgames.org) is a movement formed by gamers who are keen on pursuing the idea that games can make us into better people. These folks see games not simply as diverting amusements or propaganda but as tools that can be used to make the world a better place. One of their key voices belongs to a Portland-based author and gaming consultant, Ben Sawyer. Sawyer regularly lectures on the nature of "serious games" and the possible educational, political, and medical applications he envisions. Like other serious gamers, he is determined to show that the interactivity of games has the potential to do far more than keep a billion gamers amused in the coming decades.

I asked Sawyer whether he had encountered skepticism about the idea of serious games. After all, even I, the rambling gamers' advocate, had once doubted that games were anything more than just a great waste of time. "To some extent, yes," said Sawyer. "There are many people who have skepticism of what we're talking about. Once we spend the right amount of time, though, we usually win them over. The problem is we have to break down many misconceptions of what games are, what they can be, and how this field can be used for many different ideas and in a larger variety of ways then people first think. So it takes a while. Some of the hurdles people ask us to jump through are worthy. We shouldn't accept all serious game arguments at face value. We should earn them." But did Sawyer think that games used for educational and therapeutic purposes would change the medium's undeniably negative image? Sawyer's response was suitably cautious: "I hope it's not pitted as a 'games good for you versus games bad for you' contest. What I hope it achieves is a better perception of all the things games can be, the incredible emerging link between games and what we're learning about the brain and, in general, how we can build just new and interesting game applications."

As we've seen, advertisers, teachers, and politicians have begun to grasp some of these applications, but some of the most interesting projects to have been championed by the Serious Games Initiative were not in politics or education but in health care. Back in 2004, doctors at the University of Washington began using games as pain-relief systems for burn victims, resulting in the creation of the VR tool *Snow-World,* where kids could don a VR headset to play and escape while their wounds were treated. The creator of *Snow-World,* Dr. Hunter Hoffman, told me that the power of distraction was proving to be enormously useful in pain relief. But there were other VR implementations of gamelike technologies that also had serious applications in medical science. Hoffman explained: "For treating psychological disorders such as phobias, virtual reality helps patients confront their fears at a gradual pace they are able to tolerate. Our research suggests that phobics are much more willing to come in for VR therapy than for traditional therapy. For example, virtual spiders are fake enough that phobics will go into a virtual room with the virtual spider, when they would not go into a real world with a real spider. But the virtual spider is real enough that it elicits the responses from the patient needed for successful phobia treatment." More recently, I discovered intriguing work with VR that allowed amputee patients to visualize and "use" their phantom limbs—the nervous impulses left over from where a hand or leg had once been. Strange possibilities lie in wait as game technologies and medicine continue to converge.

Instances such as these demonstrate that games have already found some serious applications and need to be taken seriously in all walks of life. The primary purpose of all this technological innovation might have been entertainment, but the ramifications of video game technology are far greater. Does this validate all the work put into games technology? Socially useful applications of technologies that were originally developed as simply amusements have to be a good thing, don't they? For Sawyer, the discussion over the value of serious games needs to be carefully managed so that things don't get out of hand: "It would be easy to let this devolve into a bad versus good debate, but I think that itself denigrates what games are regardless of their content, and it creates a perception that somehow we [makers of serious games] are some sort of redemption. We're not. Bad games should get what they deserve: 20 percent scores in game magazines, bad sales, or thoughtful public discussion over content boundaries."

One of the places where thoughtful discussion has taken place is in the work of Gonzalo Frasca, who, with Ian Bogost (of the aforementioned Persuasive Games), discusses games with an agenda on the site Water Cooler Games (www.watercoolergames.org). This is a blog that makes the gaming fringes aware of possibilities far beyond pixelated space war and exploding monkey tennis. The authors are professionals within the game development industry and so understand both the practical and theoretical limitations of games. Their site has provided a forum for discussing a wide variety of games, from the fundamentalist religious games coming out of North America to the educational and political sex games produced by the Italian radical gamers Molleindustria. Water Cooler Games surveys the full spectrum of possibility, and the implications are occasionally profound. I asked Frasca whether he thought games were changing the world for the better. "Games can work as small laboratories for experimentation," he explained. "The gamer's attitude is different from, say, the reader's. The gamer is willing to take risks, to try new things, to explore alternative paths, to learn from others. Those are the essential skills for making social change. Certainly, a game cannot change the world in the same way that a song cannot either. A protest song can give you some ideas but the only skills that it provides are mainly singing skills. A video game can provide practical skills, problem solving, team work, analytical skills."

And yet some people still regard games as trivial. In fact, I've had discussions with tech evangelists who've suggested that the very term *games* trivializes them by associating them with toys. Frasca disagrees strongly with this: "I think that it is very dangerous to think that the term *games* trivializes the medium. What we need to do is the opposite: recognize the amazing cultural value that games have in our civilization. We do not need to try to elevate games by comparing them to other art forms: we need to learn to recognize the importance of games and toys themselves. My mantra is 'Games do not have to be fun.' Cultural products do not have to be fun. Nobody has fun with Kafka or with Bergman. Games need to be compelling, interesting, engaging. But not necessarily fun." I'm not sure I agree on the no-fun-with-Kafka angle, but Frasca has a point. It seems the only things games need to do is stave off boredom.

## AN AUDIENCE

China, Korea, and the rest of Southeast Asia's gaming population are, like me, keen to avoid being bored. And their sheer numbers make them an ever-ripening target for new waves of loaded, agenda-riddled gaming. The Chinese government's sponsorship of gaming may very well provoke another wave of patriotic feeling in China, another reason for nationalistic fervor and pride. Other gamers may succumb to different kinds of message, such as urgings to save the whales or to fight against climate change, the War on Terror, copyright constraints or infringement, or bad fashion.

In fact, I've begun to think that I missed something on my travels. Weren't games always carrying hidden agendas? How could they avoid having certain messages stitched into them? People made them, people who couldn't help but convey a few things about the world through these sophisticated constructs they had invested so much time and effort in. Okay, so perhaps *Sonic the Hedgehog* doesn't do much beyond regurgitating age-old ideas of heroism or extolling gold rings, but games are so various that the agendas range far and wide. Perhaps veteran game designer Sid Meier doesn't really believe that the wheel had to be invented at a certain stage in history, but that's what his *Civilization* games suggest. Perhaps Will Wright and Maxis Media Studios don't really believe in the value of public transport, but that's what *SimCity* teaches us.

It is widely accepted that most games come with some kind of agenda and present the world from a certain angle. They comment on or take a stand on the experiences they deliver. Writing for online games journal *The Escapist,* blogger and journalist Kieron Gillen argued that games, particularly the often neutral-sounding simulation games, were already predisposed to present the world in a certain light. He wrote: "Compare and contrast [the serious war simulation game *Operation Flashpoint*] with the recently released *Battlefield 2* demo, which posits the U.S. Marines and a Middle Eastern army as equals on a technological footage. Both are rooted in the language of the military, but they're expressing wildly separate views on the nature of a conflict. *Battlefield 2* presents a beleaguered United States in a war that is more cowboys and Indians than anything else, while [*Operation Flashpoint*] reaches for something more akin to a comment on the nature of war using theoretical examples." Is war rock and roll or hell? Does it create heroes or victims? The creators of these games get to decide. Games offer us different vantage points. As Gillen observes, "Simulation *is* expression."

Whether or not the motives of game makers mean anything to the people in the PC Baangs of South Korea, I believe that outside forces will want more than just money from them. The fantasy game world of In Sook and the other Korean gamers could eventually find itself encroached on by more than just advertising or marketing for newer and shinier games. People will want to use games— and gamers—to influence our world.

Perhaps I should mention to the paranoid reader (now likely sitting up and looking over his or her shoulder as I outline these horrors) that games have thus far at least managed to change the world in only limited ways (unless the *Legend of Zelda* series turns out to have been laced with subliminal messages that have forced us to buy two decade's worth of excessively cute Japanese video games). Producing games with a political or rhetorical bent has so far proven to be a rudimentary and unpredictable science.

Ian Bogost (himself the author of a book on games with agendas, *Persuasive Games*) had this to say of the state of the art: "There's no question that more games with a political bent appear now compared with a few years ago, but many of these games don't really make political or rhetorical statements. Instead, many are simply ordinary games with political skins or images." That hasn't stopped plenty of people from trying. Nor does it stop creators from claiming that games are expressions of personal confusion about politics or philosophy, as in the case of Ken Levine's 2007 shooter opus *BioShock,* or statements about paranoia and dissatisfaction with the government, as Harvey Smith claims for his shooter *BlackSite: Area 51.* Bogost agrees: "We are seeing more and more games that actually do use the medium's ability to model how things work to make statements about the world."

There are other, more specific examples of this: the UN Food Agency produced a game called *Food Force* that demonstrated the difficulties faced by aid agencies· in getting food to people in war-stricken areas of Africa. *Food Force*'s challenging minigames confront gamers with problems analogous to those faced by the aid workers themselves and give a limited indication of just how daunting the task can be for the everyday agency workers. Mixing limited foodstuffs in healthy amounts, finding stranded people in vast savannahs—these were tricky, occasionally haunting tasks. Free to play online, *Food Force* was one of the most downloaded games of 2006, with over seven million installations. It's a helpful educational tool if you believe that the UN is simply helping the helpless, but something far more sinister if you believe the agency has other agendas.

I asked Bogost whether he felt that projects like *Food Force* would eventually lead to mainstream games having a greater political awareness, with the gaming equivalents of

*Syriana* or *Good Night, and Good Luck* appearing on game store shelves. He responded: "I hope so, but it seems that big-budget commercial games may never get there. For all its talk about expanding the market for games, the industry doesn't seem very interested in critiquing the world—just in escaping from it." Taking a look at this week's releases, with World War II strategy games and sci-fi *Halo* wannabes dominating, it seems that Bogost is right—at least for now. What all these ideas about games changing the world seem to amount to is little more than this: the people who are creating games know that gamers are an audience and that audiences are there to be addressed.

We all want to harness other people's energies to achieve things we can't do ourselves, and games offer a particularly acute example of how this can be achieved. In "Model Living," I return in greater detail to this issue of how games and the creators of games harness gamers' creativity. But there is another, far more important point to be made here: namely, that there are subtler and more effective ways in which to harness gamers in our quest to change the world than through explicit messages alone. Game creators don't have to speak to gamers at all, nor do they necessarily have to persuade them of anything. It is by simply letting gamers get on with playing that they really begin to change the world. To me, this idea is one that seems far more radical than molding games into old-fashioned propaganda: it is the notion of using games for the purposes of "human computing."

## NINE BILLION HOURS

The concept of using games as tools for human computing is the brainchild of a young academic for whom games presently represent a sadly wasted opportunity. His

"Games with a Purpose" project aims to resolve that problem by making games do something purposeful as they entertain. Games, in his model, are tools for processing information. By his reckoning, gamers can be harnessed without any ulterior motive other than the need to process complex data.

The man is Luis von Ahn, an assistant professor at Carnegie Mellon University. He has created a series of games that use humans to resolve problems that are not currently computable using artificial processes. Von Ahn calculated that the amount of time spent by people playing the Microsoft Windows version of solitaire amounted to nine billion human hours per year. This, von Ahn suggested, represents 9 billion hours of wasted human computing. What could be accomplished by harnessing even a fraction of this, when the Panama Canal took only 20 million human hours to build?

Von Ahn set out to harness the immense lost energies of our game-playing time by looking at problems that human minds can solve but computers cannot. The first of these problems was how to label an image with a list of appropriate words. A human can look at a picture and instantly suggest single words to describe it, but a computer can't. We see this in Google's image search: the better the images are labeled, the more accurate the search facility becomes. Instead of the image search being conducted by associating an image with captions or words on the same page, it could be conducted by words that are directly associated, by human observers, with the image in question. Getting people to label images, however, would be an exorbitantly costly process. Von Ahn realized that he could create an Internet-based game, *The ESP Game,* where two people could simultaneously try to match the same words to an image. If they both got the same word, they won, and the faster they got a match, the better their score became. The two players could not communicate other than to know that the other had made a guess. The players could only type single words and try to match them with their unseen partner. There was no other mode of interaction. Despite this, players of the game knew there was another person playing, and many gamers reported feeling a connection when someone came up with a similar esoteric description. This feeling—this tiny sliver of empathy via electronic equipment—added to the already compulsive nature of the game and made it an online smash hit.

Collecting the most consistent results from the thousands of sessions of *The ESP Game* allowed von Ahn's team to accurately label images with lists of words. If you want a picture with a dog and flower in it, you're far more likely to get hold of it if the file you are searching has been labeled using von Ahn's methods. Without a solution like *The ESP Game,* such image labeling would have been financially impossible, but as it is, the service is free.

The most important feature of von Ahn's invention is that it is fun: people enjoy playing the image-labeling game and want to do it. Through a little insight into what motivates gamers, as well as some clever design, von Ahn was able to harness gamers' boundless energies. He created a free image-labeling service thanks to human computing.

One of the unforeseen ramifications of this method was that it allowed pictures to make sense to readers designed to read Web sites for blind people: when a reader reaches an image, it could, thanks to this application, go some way toward describing it, rather than simply reading the attached caption aloud. Using similar techniques and another game, Von Ahn has gone on to examine ways of identifying the location of specific objects within images. Von Ahn has started to show us that there are many possible applications for human computing though games, and most of these are yet to be discovered.

## NEW PATTERNS

It's at this point that I begin to become uncomfortable. I indicated in the previous section that I believe that games already have a purpose, without von Ahn having to invent one. To entertain should be purpose enough. But what if von Ahn is right? What if the human hours of millions upon millions of gamers across Europe, America, and Asia can be gradually harnessed to computational ends? Human computing through gaming could become a major force in changing the world for the better. Our shiny supercomputing future might achieve its most practical results not by using faster processors but by harnessing (distributed) human intelligence for a specific goal. We're already seeing the power of conventional distributed computing in projects like SETI@home; what if visionaries such as von Ahn were able to come up with even more formidable applications for idle human minds? Are we going to find our gaming activities colluding with game creators on more than just entertainment? Von Ahn himself is confident of this future and sees the possibilities as limitless.

Yet this prospect makes me shiver. Von Ahn's description of hours spent gaming as "wasted human cycles" has a vaguely Orwellian ring to it. There are no such vibes from the man himself, who is enormously intelligent, charming, and gracious. Still, the "Games with a Purpose" project seems to me to go against the spirit of the gaming I've enjoyed over the last couple of decades. Von Ahn's approach to gaming assumes that it somehow wastes otherwise useful time. Guiltily, I think about the hours I pumped into creating a Dwarf Paladin at level 50-something in *World of*

*Warcraft,* and I feel like he's right. But perhaps I only feel this way because I am shut off and distant from the experience and the game I was playing at the time. Perhaps if I was right there, caught in the heat of a battle with my gaming companions, I'd be able to dismiss the feeling. Yet the suspicion remains: just how much time has been lost? In short, the guilty possibility still looms: gaming isn't saving the world; it's just wasting time—just another slacker project with no outcome, no utility, no greater good. Perhaps we're even dooming ourselves in some unforeseeable way—a youth spent in obsessive gaming delivering us brain ailments that are as yet unidentified and unforeseen.

Some commentators have drawn even more unsettling conclusions about our time spent playing games. An article published in the *Wilson Quarterly* (an anthology that reprints an editor's selection of general interest articles from various media outlets in each issue) suggests that games were actually making gamers into more obedient, more pliable servants of "the system." The author, Chris Suellentrop, concludes: "Whether you find the content of video games inoffensive or grotesque, their structure teaches players that the best course of action is always to accept the system and work to succeed within it. . . . Gamers are famous for coming up with creative approaches to the problems a game presents. But devising a new, unexpected strategy to succeed under the existing rules isn't the same thing as proposing new rules, new systems, or new patterns." The danger of games, Suellentrop suggests, is that they teach us that success means discovering and then following the rules—a deeper genre of propaganda. If he's right, then the ever-growing millions of obsessed gamers could eventually be playing their way into a new and subtle kind of oppression, something far more worrying than finding their "wasted cycles" put to use in the technology of a major corporation's search engine.

Could gaming be not the opium of the masses but the prescribed sedative? What better way to deal with a bored, alienated population than to invent the perfect distraction? Why not allow them to escape, all the time? Isn't that what all leisure has really been about: keeping us quiet and just happy enough so that we don't bother to worry about the big picture?

Suellentrop's essay certainly struck a chord with me. Perhaps there really is a darker core to our brave new world of entertainment. Perhaps games foster a sheeplike conformity. But I don't think so. I believe that gamers are finding their own purposes for games and are proposing new rules, new systems, and new patterns rather than docilely following the established ones. You might not be able to change the physics from within a game, but that doesn't mean you can't have the game changed. Gamers can and do subvert games, and, as I'll report later on, many of them exercise a cruel, anarchic, punk ethic in doing so. They're not motivated by any outside political agenda or because they want to save the world; they're doing it because they want to be entertained. If you talk to any gamer about the games they play, they're likely to have ideas about how they could be radically different or what alterations would be really cool. And this all comes down to one thing that games really do feed in us: imagination.

◄ REYKJAVIK ►

# The Special Relationship

EVOLUTIONARY CHANGE

The success of my *Quake* team didn't last. About a year after my new job started, we began to break up and drift apart. It wasn't just us, either. The *Quake III* scene was beginning to fade across Europe, as new games were released and old communities began to lose their collective enthusiasm. Some of the people from the team were already getting involved in other online games, such as the pseudomedieval wars of *Dark Age of Camelot* and the bite-sized World War II escapades of *Battlefield 1942*. Eventually we decided to end it.

Mildly despondent, I found solace in off-line games, work, and writing a terrible novel about sentient graffiti. I yearned for the camaraderie and the conflict that running the team had provided. And the void the team had left didn't seem to fade or to be filled up with other projects. I began to dabble in other online games, but none of them really suited my method of play. The entire world seemed to be in the thrall of the team-based combat of *Counter-Strike,* with its counterterrorism theme and realistic weapons. But it just didn't suit me. I no longer felt part of a community.

One of the games I began to experiment with during that time was called *EVE Online*. I loved the massively multiplayer concept it offered: thousands of people playing side by side in a vast, persistent galaxy. Trade, fight, build spaceships, and then fly them through the heavens—it was just the kind of gaming concept and fiction I could invest in. The only problem was that I didn't really understand how it all worked. Grabbing a rocket launcher and defending a flag I understood. But trading on virtual markets, mining rocks, and fitting out fictional starships with a hundred different pieces of equipment? Well, that was too much for me. I soon gave up and looked for my fun elsewhere.

A couple of months later, I was back in *EVE* again, this time on the promise of a friend who was playing the game. He claimed that we'd be able to set up and run a mercenary company within the game world. We'd be bounty hunters, taking on contracts and hunting down villains for cash. It sounded thrilling. It became obvious quite soon that there was one crucial problem: we had no more idea how to become bounty hunters in this game than we did in real life. After a couple of months of floundering and aimless hours of exploring, we finally caught and killed our first miscreant. But he was also our last. I gave up on *EVE* and started playing other games.

And yet again, I was enticed back. My first two forays had imbued this game with a sense of mystery: how could a game be so complex that its workings were beyond my appraisal, even after weeks of play? What was it about this space game that made me return, despite the fact that I'd been so bored, frustrated, and perplexed? I began trying to answer some of these questions in an article. I discussed what it was that made this game unique, how it offered possibilities and choices rather than quests and stories. I began to see how it wasn't "virtual" as such but, as Steven Shaviro describes cyberspace in his book *Connected*, "prosthetic." *EVE* was an extension of what I was doing in my everyday life. It was hard work. Commitment.

Eventually it was also rewarding. I documented all this in my article "All about *EVE*," which was eventually published in the popular U.K. magazine *PC Gamer*. A number of people who read the article wanted me to help them access the game, as I'd been helped by other members of its community. I found myself setting up an in-game corporation, hiring people I knew from Internet forums or from work, and helping them decide how to make the most out of the choices that this pretend galaxy offered them.

The psychic hole left by the end of my *Quake* years had been filled, without me even realizing it had happened. I'm still helping to run that *EVE* corporation today. I'm also still trying to figure out just what this strange game's appeal is for me and to document the ways in which it has inspired gamers like me to do unexpected things. Part of that project of documentation meant traveling to where the game was conceived, designed, and created. And so I headed off to Reykjavik, the capital city of a tiny nation in the North Atlantic: Iceland.

## THE *STAR WARS* MACHINE

Years of climate-destroying international travel have turned me into a connoisseur of Heathrow Airport's long gray carpets. I've become familiar with each of the four terminals and now realize that each of them has a subtle and distinct flavor. Despite the uniform flooring materials and the themed sequence of corporate placards it shares with all the other buildings, Terminal 2 is a little more haphazard than the other flight-boarding structures. On a cold day in November 2006, it seemed altogether less organized—and perhaps less restrained and more relaxed—than the other terminals. None of the others, for example, had a *Star Wars* arcade cabinet of 1983 vintage resting halfway down the concourse.

The bulky, old-fashioned cabinet had been weathered by time, but it was nevertheless plugged in and functional. The game stood out like a beacon or a waypoint, and the fact that it rested next to the gate through which I was set to depart seemed auspicious. The cabinet was waiting there for a customer, silently, as it likely had done in other locations for the past twenty years. Wandering past the grubby TV screen, I suppressed my puppyish urge to rush over and pump the cabinet's large plastic buttons. Instead I sat down to wait for the Icelandair flight to Reykjavik. From a distance, I watched the faint head-up display lines of an X-Wing plunge down a Death Star's equatorial trench as the game played along by itself. The flickering display presented a simplified interpretation of the final space battle scenes of the first *Star Wars* movie; it was a sequence that must have played itself out on that screen many tens of thousands of times before.

Dotted between the roller-necked business travelers were dozens of young men wearing T-shirts emblazoned with twenty-first-century remixes of 1980s gaming icons. Some T-shirts displayed visual puns, images that combined jargonized witticisms, or jokes cobbled together from Internet neologisms. Others bore profane acronyms and absurd emoticons. Others still were deliberately outlandish: pink, lime green, furnished with the logo of the Bank of Alabama. By and large these travelers were an older generation of gamer, 20- or 30-somethings who were highly computer literate. Many of them no doubt harbored expansive knowledge of gaming ephemera and would almost certainly have seen the *Star Wars* machine through my eyes. Eventually I noticed that one young man in an Atari T-shirt was watching the *Star Wars* machine's silent sequence. He leaned forward in his seat. Mentally I urged him to get up and play on the machine, since I was too embarrassed to do so. And eventually, to my surprise and joy, he did just that.

Video games make up a teeming mass of contemporary popular culture, of which past *Star Wars* games are now fading icons. Thousands of games have been produced since that *Star Wars* cabinet first appeared, but some of them, like the *Star Wars* franchise in general, enjoy a peculiar social and cultural gravitas. The great games are the exceptions, milestones, iconoclasts, innovators—and the most important of them stand out as psychic landmarks for the gamers who played them. The name *Tempest* might sound Shakespearean to those who are unfamiliar with the 1980s electronic entertainment, but for many gamers—those who have been locked in its pixelated tunnels—it refers to a single, legendary arcade game that none of them is likely ever to forget. Like reading a great work of literature or becoming hooked on a particular wave of pop records, playing these masterwork games has defined our worldviews, filled out our vocabularies, and shaped our personalities. That *Star Wars* machine would, I knew, have featured prominently in the past of someone, somewhere—perhaps it even represented their first encounter with a video game.

I poured these thoughts into my notebook, each one seeming a little more plausible as I scribbled. For the past decade, I had been reading seemingly endless reports about gamers and the various fruits of their hyperactivity—a man killed for stealing an in-game item, a video game played on stage at a heavy metal concert, countless people meeting in games and falling in love. Games had turned into econ-

omies, political criticism, costume party cliques, and Hollywood films whose values were to be contested in a boxing
match. (Uwe Boll, maker of terrible films based on video
game licenses, fought some of his critics in a bizarre
arranged duel in Vancouver.) My friends and colleagues
filed reports of gaming obsessions from the Ukraine, China,
Brazil, or California, all of them detailing the ideas and activities that games were generating, spontaneously, as in
some vast, distributed conversation. And here I was, heading off to a volcanic landmass in the freezing North Atlantic to drink and eat and party, all for the sake of gaming.

## HYPERMODERNIZED VIKING

Iceland is a beautiful raw place, burned into the North Atlantic by restless geology. On a bleak November afternoon,
the clouds were low and the rain continuous, but the dead
grass, gray skies, and empty black barrens of volcanic rock
were nevertheless awesome. The taxi driver's radio played
a mix of peculiar honking and kitsch Icelandic sing-along
tunes. It conjured images of men in knitted sweaters, mid-
dling keyboard players with a mission to inject pop into traditional Scandinavian music—a Scandinavian equivalent of
the sad attempts to update, for example, American country
music by mangling it into modern pop songs. My heart
sank as I noticed the astronomical figure on the meter as
we approached the outskirts of Reykjavik, a city in which
there had been no trees until 1986.

Reykjavik has the characteristics of many coastal towns
of the far north: windswept buildings built for the cold, often with corrugated materials and sharply sloped roofs.
This hypermodernized Viking outpost also has one of the

most advanced technology infrastructures on earth. It has the highest number of broadband Internet connections per capita of any OECD country, and its outlying winter landscape is punctuated by the glow of geoelectrically fueled sunlamps that feed vast, fruit-swollen greenhouses on the volcanic marches. Reykjavik is a midpoint between Europe and America, and its architecture, automobiles, and merchandise are an interesting mix of the two continents. Broad American cars, so incongruous in mainland Europe, inhabit the streets alongside familiar jelly-mold Fiats and Skodas.

Iceland also has a vibrant esoteric pop culture. One of its most famous exports is the singer-songwriter Bjork, whose singular voice and experimental attitudes have sold 15 million records worldwide. The tiny singer is a perfect ambassador for the island nation: exuberant, fierce, and unusual. The country's other cultural exports are equally iconoclastic and remarkably unconstrained by the preconceptions that seem to burden cultural projects in other countries. The children's TV show *LazyTown*, which is currently being shown in 98 countries worldwide, is produced in Icelandic studios using a mixed cast of American and Icelandic actors, CGI, and traditional artistry. The show is crammed with weird hyperactivity, melding a mix of real-world props with computer-generated environments and actors. A perfect example of Iceland's topped-out tech level, *LazyTown* employs a large swathe of the most technically proficient designers and engineers in Reykjavik. It is also one of the most expensive children's television series ever to be produced. Its immense popularity seems to depend as much on cash-fueled technological complexity as it does on the charm and energy of its star and creator, the fitness guru Magnús Scheving. The almost alarming zaniness of this half-hour show may seem to be an unlikely product of the long dark winters of Iceland, but it is suffused with the rich humor and outward-looking attitude that defines the national culture.

Another, equally offbeat product of the North Atlantic is the game that I was on my way to see. *EVE Online* is Iceland's other hi-tech progeny: a critically lauded online world with its own full-time economist and a 200,000-strong population of gamers. Like Iceland itself, the game is an acquired taste and the preferred destination for a limited number of travelers. It, too, is bleakly beautiful and as technologically sophisticated as it is forbidding and cruel. It is a game that could only have been made here in this mid-Atlantic bubble, where certain rules do not seem to apply. It was a debut project that seemed completely uncowed by the considerable risks it was taking. CCP, the company behind *EVE,* was unrelenting in the face of commercial pressures, they were also, like the Vikings, pioneering and perhaps even foolhardy. This game has been hugely controversial and has attracted a peculiar kind of commitment from its players—of which I am one particularly troubled example. I love this game, and I loathe it.

My first glimpse of *EVE* happened after a magazine editor dismissed it as doomed. It was something that either would never be commercially released or would disappear into the gaming churn without a trace within a few months, just another overly optimistic project lost to bad luck and bad marketing—or so the editor predicted. But instead of vanishing, it consolidated, grew, expanded, and inspired. Reykjavik's hi-tech baby had obsessed me for five years. Arriving at its home gave me a sense of energy that was inaccessible elsewhere. I was heading toward the source of a gaming project that had consumed a significant portion of my life.

EIGHTIES AMOEBA

Later that afternoon, I crossed a second long gray carpet, this one in the hotel bar of the convention center hosting the *EVE* festival. There on the refined flooring of the Nordica Hotel, I delivered my thoughts about the *Star Wars* machine to one of Reykjavik's 300,000 citizens. He sat staring off intently in a way that made me wonder whether he was really listening. But eventually he laughed. "The original Death Star run?" he asked, clearly incredulous. I nodded. "We should get one of those!" It was this man's game I had come to Reykjavik to discuss. *EVE Online* is unlikely ever to retire to the corner of an airport lounge, precisely because its exploding starships exist in a networked place quite different from that of the old arcade machines: the Internet.

*EVE Online* seems a galaxy far, far away from the crude polygonal vectors of the 1983 *Star Wars*. It's glistening spacecraft and dark nebulae transmit something utterly modern and uniquely imagined, though the evolutionary line that runs between it and the *Star Wars* machine can still be quite clearly defined. If one were so inclined, it would be possible to map a genealogy of computer space combat, starting out in the 1960s with *Spacewar,* visiting *Space Invaders* at the end of the 1970s, and buying into the *Star Wars* arcade game in the early 1980s. We might then see the idea expand geometrically through the space trading game *Elite* at the end of the Thatcher-Reagan era and evolve through *Elite*'s many imitators across the 1990s. (There are some weird sideshows as time goes on—such as the Hollywood-obsessed *Wing Commander* games.) Then, finally, as the millennium approached, the genre catalyzed into something new: the advent of accelerated graphics and the Internet brought us *EVE Online*. Here, at the end of our chronology, is the space game in its most sophisticated incarnation. Iceland's most advanced product brings us up to date: this is twenty-first-century networked space war.

Games like the one in the *Star Wars* box have been casting ripples through the gene pool of 20 years of accelerating technology. Although contemporary games might seem like multicellular monstrosities by comparison to these early amoeba of the 1980s, their basic makeup is the same. *EVE Online* is about flying a starship, blowing things up, and defeating your enemy—just like the *Star Wars* game. In the Icelandic version, however, we play a game of starships and space stations with a concurrent population of up to 35,000 other people from across the world.

There had been similarly lavish-looking space games before, but *EVE* took things a step further by using the technology pioneered by games like *EverQuest* and *Ultima Online* to connect thousands of people to a single game world via the Internet. *EVE*'s players shoot not only at computer-generated enemies but also at each other. They are free to fight or flee, to talk or trade; and unlike the *Star Wars* machine, there is no one sequence that can be played over and over. It is continuous, changing, and fluid. *EVE*'s population of 35,000 draws on a combined pool of 150,000 subscribers, each of whom pay $15 each month for constant access to the *EVE* universe. This is far from our 20 minutes of five-a-side *Quake* combat, where the arena reset once victory was achieved. Instead *EVE* is persistent, expansive, and evolving, with thousands of players competing and cooperating in an ongoing game.

Loading up *EVE* gives you access to a trio of spacefaring characters, a hangar full of spaceships, and a market economy in which only the most ruthless will become rich and famous. It's a rich, dark world, with design reminiscent of David Lynch's sci-fi movie *Dune*. You pilot your ship from a third-person perspective, guiding it between celestial waypoints, such as space stations and stargates. Drop-down menus reveal possible interactions—chat, shoot, orbit, approach. The game exudes a kind of deliberate functional indifference. Like an operating system for the heavens, it challenges you to learn how to use it. Knowing what the thousands of equipment items and hundreds of starships do is an education in itself. Learning which human pilots are your friends and which are betrayers is crucial. This is a game that does not offer objectives or easy goals, it simply offers itself: a dangerous, malevolent space in which to work.

These kinds of projects have been called "virtual worlds"—online 3-D spaces where our gaming alter egos can grow and be developed over time and where the world carries on even when the home computer is turned off. *EverQuest, World of Warcraft, Ultima Online, Second Life*—all these games have achieved fame and fortune via the virtual world idea. Compared to them, *EVE* is an obscure, unapproachable corner of the online scene, overshadowed utterly by the commercial successes of its peers. It is, however, also one of *the* important games, one of the landmarks I spoke of earlier. It is important not because of its (lack of) popularity but because it has enabled gamers to do things that they could not do before and cannot do anywhere else.

## MEDIEVAL EUROPE

*EVE* enabled me to build up a team of people whose gaming talents and interests all complemented each other. Our efforts would persist within the game world and be written into its history. We would work hard to be an autonomous unit, so that even when we joined up with larger alliances of players, our little corporation would be able to look after itself: our talent as pilots has been something to be proud of. Our real achievements, however, were to be found in the name we made for ourselves and the reputation we earned with other players. A persistent character with genuinely valuable virtual inventory might be one reason why players feel attached to their time in *EVE*, but it's the social mesh that really hooked me. As in life, what has come to matter within the *EVE* universe are our relationships with other people—how they feel toward us and whether we are to be trusted or feared.

*EVE*'s universe consists of a single cluster of computers. This network of machines is where *EVE*'s universe actually exists, and it is what gamers are accessing when they play the game. Unlike other online games, which usually host many different, cloned instances of their online world, *EVE Online* is a single virtual galaxy, hosted by a single group of machines. Much like the real galaxy, this one constitutes a work in progress. It changes, grows, and (perhaps unlike our galaxy) occasionally goes haywire.

Day-to-day progress is propelled by the game's complex cash economy and the robust infrastructure that the players have built over time. *EVE*'s in-game economy is equivalent to that of a small town, with the databases and market systems required to support the virtual businesses of its gamers. Its inhabitants make friends and enemies, fight, build, and make money. The marketing mythology surrounding *EVE* boasts that a demo of the game at an economic forum in Reykjavik had visiting American professors raving about the way it demonstrated their theories of microeconomics. Perhaps these professors asked their students to play the game so that they might better grasp the theories they were studying. If any of them did so, they would have discovered a remarkably feudal in-game social system, with players forming warring tribes and dealing with each other in a barbarous, violent manner—a space-bound medieval Europe. *EVE*'s sophisticated virtual economy is fueled by one thing: war. Millions of transactions and interactions take place each day, each one seeking ways to support the huge military economies. CCP takes this economic complex so seriously that they've hired a full-time economist to deliver quarterly reports on the galactic economy—just as banks and governments do as they audit economic activities of real countries.

*EVE*'s endless conflicts give the game a kind of semifictional history. It's "semifictional" because the gamers who play in it aren't exactly acting, and the history they share results from real human interaction as much as it does from the background story developed by the game's creators. The history of *EVE* is fashioned just as real history is fashioned—through the experience of real people. For every story of sci-fi conflict penned by a game designer, there are a hundred stories of gamers scamming other gamers or brave player-pilots winning battles against the odds. My own love for the game came not from the fictions that the game creators had crafted but from the stories I was able to tell of my own accomplishments: foes bested, alliances forged, spaceships produced.

These days, the job of *EVE*'s creators is to burn new layers of detail into the galaxy through successive changes to the computer code that constitutes it. Gamers meanwhile get on with populating and using the *EVE* world. They engage in war; exploration; economics; politics; trade; manufacturing; construction; and, occasionally, entertainment.

For all these reasons and more, *EVE* has thrilled, frustrated, appalled, and delighted me. And it has, more than any previous game, focused and motivated me. By the end of 2006, I had given up numerous times, returning after a few months, when I was unable to find the same satisfaction in other games. I knew that if I was going to sink this much time into a game, I wanted it to count for something, for it to involve people I felt a connection with; I wanted to play with people who understood why I couldn't give it up and who wanted more than just a series of interesting choices.

And so I had arrived from Heathrow along with five hundred other gamers and journalists. For identification purposes, many people wore T-shirts proclaiming their in-game allegiance. Others arrived in costume or wore outlandish goth uniforms—incongruous in the foyer of sandstone and faux marble. In shirt and cheap jeans, I remained anonymous.

The man I had been talking to at the *EVE* event about my airport encounter with the *Star Wars* machine was anonymous to no one. He was an event celebrity: Nathan Richardsson, the senior producer of *EVE Online*. And after listening to my story of the errant arcade machine, he got back to the subject at hand: changes to the *EVE* system.

*EVE Online* does not (cannot) remain static, and it is Richardsson's job to decide what must be changed. The bearded Icelander revealed that one of the game's basic systems was to be radically altered in the next update of the world. It was a function of movement, something that had not, in all the years of the game's life span, functioned as intended. Originally, celestial objects could not be flown to at warp speed and instead had to be approached from a distance. Now, with the latest change, you would arrive next to them. I was pleased to hear it would be fixed, but Richardsson seemed glum. Why? Even minor alterations were a difficult matter for him, and this one had clearly been agonized over at length. But there was nevertheless more to it than that.

The change had to do with the way players had learned

to move their spaceships from place to place, and it was going to damage one of the possible player moneymaking activities. Players had discovered that they were able to use in-game monetary systems to sell the coordinates within space that allowed for safe traveling. Rather than warping to a celestial object and then trundling the last few miles, you could warp to a player-made coordinate that was already a few miles behind your target and thereby land on top of it. These spatial coordinates cold be sold as in-game files, and subsequently the bookmark makers were able to generate huge profits for their work. The players had worked this out without any help from the developers, and the system had not even been foreseen by the developers when the game had been put together. Players had figured out the best ways to transfer the coordinates, and the cash generated was adding to the thriving in-game economy. Sadly, however, the bookmarks had begun to affect the performance of the game, since they began to proliferate in the tens of thousands.

Of course, this was rather like a caretaker of the laws of a universe having to make a minor change that would directly interfere with its inhabitants—like God reaching down to make sure that train timetables were never invented. Richardsson lamented having to disable any activity that the players had come up with by themselves, especially one like this. It was one of the many "emergent" possibilities generated by the activities of *EVE* players. And emergence was what made *EVE* worth playing.

## CHANGING ROOMS

The concept of emergence is central to all kinds of gaming discussion. Even when it is not mentioned specifically, it is implicit in much of what gamers like to talk about. In its most basic sense, "emergence" refers to the way that a small set of rules can generate a highly complex set of consequences. *SimCity,* for example, presents us with a limited number of tools for building a city and a series of easy rules for using them. The uncontrollable explosion of events that result from the players' road building and industry zoning nevertheless presents us with a complicated, emergent situation that requires serious struggle to master. In short, emergent games are ones that allow a huge range of possibilities and don't dictate a strict, linear flow of events.

A strategy game is emergent because so many units can interact and have some effect on each other. There are so many possible interactions between individual game entities that the games can generate immensely complex, often surprising results. What is crucial about these results is that they become intelligible only through the act of actually playing the game. Gamers learn how a game functions by playing it—not by reading the manual or by hearing descriptions from other gamers. In fact, no one can say for sure how a game will work until it has been played by real people, no matter how well they understand the basic rules. Emergent games are said to be "computationally irreducible," because the consequences of playing them cannot be deduced through any analytical shortcut. And that's why commercial games are played so extensively by games testers in the final stages of development: the programmers might have had a perfect understanding of everything they did to make the system, but they cannot predict exactly how a game will be used. Understanding how the programming rules function can only be understood in the process of playing the game itself.

The activity of gaming is filled with examples of emergence in action. What I find even more fascinating, though, is the way in which emergent games inspire the emergent behavior of gamers themselves—the unique and peculiar things gamers will do with a game. As we'll see, the emergent possibilities created by certain games have enabled gamers to undertake some unexpected projects. Situations that were unforeseen by game designers are routinely created by imaginative gaming, and it is these unintended consequences that I want to explore. I also want to see how, at least in the case of *EVE,* some players deliberately set out to create new and unforeseen situations.

The American game designer Harvey Smith described one of the most famous examples of unexpected emergent behavior. Harvey's example—the so-called proximity mine problem—grew out of his open-ended action shooter masterpiece *Deus Ex,* but it illustrates the kind of thing that gamers get up to on a routine basis: "Some clever players figured out that they could attach a proximity mine to the wall and hop up onto it (because it was physically solid and therefore became a small ledge, essentially). So then these players would attach a second mine a bit higher, hop up onto the prox mine, reach back and remove the first proximity mine, replace it higher on the wall, hop up one step higher, and then repeat, thus climbing any wall in the game, escaping our carefully predefined boundaries." ("Escaping our carefully predefined boundaries" sounds like a slogan that should be on the T-shirts of traveling gamers.) Most gamers are familiar with similar kinds of stories. These kinds of situation are routine, especially in their online games modes, where gamers are able to work together to perform feats that were clearly not intended to be part of the game. Emergent behavior can take many forms, from action game players standing on each other's heads to create exploding towers of people, to simply figuring out the best mode of cooperating to kill a tough opponent.

Moments before writing this paragraph, I was part of an

online conversation with another game journalist, Quintin Smith. It was a typical exchange of gaming lore, and it left me with a snapshot of emergent fun as it happens in the wild. Smith had been playing an action game, *Thievery*, which is based around stealth and stealing. Players form opposing teams of thieves and guards and sneak and patrol against each other. The thieves, of course, must loot, while the guards are out to catch them. But it wasn't the larcenous aims of the game that had made that evening's play so entertaining; it was the interior decoration. "There were rudimentary physics and a lot of items scattered about," said Smith. "One map had a huge manor that the thief side were meant to loot, but it also had a small bar in the corner. During one cooperative match, we began ignoring loot and collecting household furniture to turn the bar into a den. Medieval larceny became *Changing Rooms*." (*Changing Rooms* is an inexplicably popular British TV program about household furnishing.) Smith's thievery was at least temporarily forgotten because the game world had suddenly provided another possibility. The players had used the character's in-game skills to creep about, dragging around furniture that was entirely incidental to the theft mission. Placing stools and tables, mugs and jugs, had become the new, unspecified goal of the game. Silly, yes, but the very fact that it was possible, unintended, and original to these players made it more amusing, more entertaining, than the game in hand. The experience might always have been about exploring, experimenting, and playing, but here were a bunch of players subverting the rules and conventions they were supposed to follow, in order to cook up a completely different way of being entertained. It happens all the time.

Smith's anecdote about *Changing Rooms* demonstrates just how unpredictable the human element of a game really is. Of course, this kind of behavior is not peculiar to games; once people are given tools, they will always find new uses for them—it's simply in our nature to improvise and invent as we play. There are, however, serious differences of opinion about what this kind of behavior means: is emergent play simply the passing enjoyment of novelty? Perhaps it is, but there are more complex examples—what might be called "emergent projects"—that suggest that emergence does something more for gamers than simply supply us with a few surprises. Some emergence involves less trivial goals, including the kinds of socioeconomic process that require years of careful cooperation and formidable willpower to accomplish. But I'll come back to that in a few paragraphs' time.

## ASTEROIDS

Returning to Reykjavik and to Richardsson, it's clear that he and his team have always expected their players to "break out of predefined boundaries." Since its earliest days, *EVE* has benefited from the seemingly endless inventiveness of gamers. In fact, *EVE* was originally intended to be a game of economics and resources, complete with market information, trading tools, production facilities, and consumer items; but quite how all these elements would come together wasn't immediately clear. The wealth of resources seemed bound to give rise to some kind of emergent behavior, since players would almost certainly find uses for them that the game creators had not foreseen. As in any other real-world economy, people would find novel ways of getting hold of cash, just because they could. (For example, a beggar I followed traveling from one solar system to the next would ask local pilots for the game equivalent of "just $10,000," adding, "because I need to raise

$100,000." In reality, this was barely a few cents. Wealthy pilots would feel pity and cough up the $100K. The beggar then moved on to the next system. . . .) It was impossible for *EVE*'s designers to predict exactly what gamers might end up discovering, so complex were the possibilities they had created. However, for *EVE* to be interesting at all, it would require players to find interesting ways to behave. Fortunately they did just that from the outset, and in the early days, it was all to do with rocks.

One of the in-game resources that *EVE*'s players keenly exploit are asteroids, which can be "mined" for mineral reward. Of course, asteroids are just one of a number of resources that *EVE*'s creators provided at the outset. But what they hadn't foreseen was the patience with which players would mine these space rocks or the way that the rocks enabled some players to become astronomically wealthy within just a few weeks of the game's launch. What had happened was that the earliest adopters had discovered a loophole in the way the game worked, an unintended function of cargo canisters that made their mining unexpectedly efficient. While mining ships were supposed to travel back to base each time a cargo hold was filled, the player discovered that they could eject cargo cans next to their ship, thus increasing their storage capacity immensely and making the space rock easier to haul back at a later time. It had never been intended as such, but suddenly *EVE Online* was the game about farming space minerals. Players had once again climbed outside the predefined boundaries, and in a matter of days, they had transformed *EVE* from role-playing action game to a space-mining management simulation. It is a reputation the game has never quite managed to shrug off.

Asteroid harvesting was only ever intended to have niche appeal, and its initial popularity was entirely unanticipated by *EVE*'s creators. But although the game's focus soon returned to shooting, the mining bug never went away. In fact, *EVE*'s design team was delighted by it: mining meant cooperation. Players would have to work together to get rich. Instead of designers erasing the loophole and forcing players to get on with shooting each other or trading in consumer goods, this new way of mining was written into the game and further facilitated in later iterations of the game code. By working out how to "break" the game, players had changed its direction forever. It was as if Smith's in-game furnishing had been extrapolated into a subgame of interior decoration, with the game's creators providing the option for wallpaper and a comfy sofa.

Reactions to player behavior were to shape much of the overall direction of *EVE* in the years that followed. Although the game's creators could predict how many of the more mechanical elements of the game would work, the human side had to be studied in the field. The team had always intended players to fight each other for control of territory, as they did from day one, but even as I write these words, the problem of turning territorial conflict into a functional gaming system has not been resolved. The things that made *EVE* such an appealing game also made it into an intractable design problem: how far could they let players go, and could anyone ever actually be allowed to "win"? How do you create a game that functions at once as a battleground, à la *Star Wars,* and a satisfying outing for a couple of friends wanting to explore the galaxy? These are ongoing problems for a small army of game designers.

The programmers, meanwhile, are busy providing tools that allow better man management, so that people can organize groups of tens, hundreds, or thousands of other players. They've even managed to implement contract systems that allow players to earn trust in a financial world where there is no genuine liability for one's actions. All of this represents unprecedented terrain for gaming, and yet still the game is awkward, unfinished, unresolved. We can get on with the business of playing, enjoying the combat, trade, and exploration, but it's always going to change. It has to change and has been doing so for over three years. And still hard problems remain: how much freedom can you give to 150,000 players? How do you balance the power of hundreds and thousands of people in a single game? "We've got a lot of work still to do," says Richardsson, a man who knows that *EVE* is more an ongoing experiment in game design than the definitive space war.

By "we," Richardsson might of course have been referring to the players as well as the designers. As much as the team of programmers and artists create, it's ultimately down to the gamers to play and play. The game slowly changes in light of what they achieve. *EVE* is their work in progress as much as it is a decadelong quest for its creators. This unusual relationship will likely continue until all the players leave and the stars shut down. These people need each other, symbiotically. It is not even as if the game could now be mothballed and then revived and dusted off at a later date. *EVE* is alive because of how players bought into it and how creators worked on it from day to day. Picking up *EVE* isn't like picking up the Game Boy you bought ten years ago for a quick burst of *Tetris*. You log out of *EVE* knowing it won't be the same when you return. *EVE*, more than any other game out there, is an event.

Such player activities as selling the travel coordinates might have broken Richardsson's game by overloading the coordinate-handling server, but coming up with them in the first place was the whole point of what CCP was trying to achieve. They wanted to make their model so open-ended that people had to figure out their own solutions for problems. Buying and loading coordinates drew you into the emergent aspects of the game—without them, you were a second-rate pilot. Such exploratory behavior was utterly vital to the success of *EVE*, and without it, there would have been an enormous amount of stagnation. Instead of having to be a director waving a magic wand that orchestrated every nuance of every experience within the game universe, Richardsson and his team could rely on gamers to make their own progress and their own entertainment.

*EVE* players can contribute in all kinds of ways. They can contribute through politics, wars, trade agreements, and mutual pacts. They create wars and peace accords. They find new ways to use what the game has given them and to generate activities that were unforeseen by anyone else. *EVE* pilots organize their own entertainment: several spaceship races, for example. These were impromptu solar system rallies, where various speeding ships were able to compete for prizes by rigging their ships for speed and then hurtling through the void. Other players used the monetary systems to organize lotteries of virtual cash. Events like these were entirely unscripted and unsupported by the designers. All Richardsson and his team had needed to do was build the framework, then, like gods sitting back to watch their pocket universe, they could watch it perform. There are gamers who run Internet radio stations broadcasting music, news, and sometimes "travel reports" based on dangers reported within the game world. Perhaps most impressive of all are the players who worked out how to develop games-within-games for *EVE*'s in-game browser. This simple tool for viewing Web pages had been included to allow gamers to create out-of-game Web sites for their corporations and alliances, but it was soon put to other uses. By figuring out how to make this in-game browser (which cannot browse normal Web pages) host an online poker tournament or multiplayer *Connect Four*, enterprising *EVE* players had given the general population of players something else to do in-game, ensuring that they weren't going to get bored while they were gnawing at space rocks.

There have been darker ramifications, too. Scamming has been rife, with the largest player-run "investment opportunity" turning out to be a fairly sophisticated pyramid scheme, with large dividends paid back using subsequent investments. The organizer claimed to have run off with the virtual equivalent of around $100,000. It was all legitimate, said the developers. You have to be smart to survive. Other gamers were banned for "exploits" that were abuses of the many loopholes the programmers had been unable to foresee or fix.

These remarkably lifelike possibilities arise from the rules of the game but are also born of the creativity and ingenuity of gamers. We are so keen to find ways of keeping *EVE* fresh and challenging that the game necessarily develops in unforeseen directions. When a game environment is as complex as this, it becomes increasingly likely that unpredictable circumstances will emerge. We want them to emerge, and we make it happen. And yet all this takes place within the boundaries of what we recognize as a game. *EVE* is not some simulatory oddity, an operating system, or a 3-D building program. It is a vast universe populated by computer-controlled enemies, space stations, weird mutant drone machines, hidden asteroid belts, and human players in ships of various kinds. It is not a game in which mastery with a gun will ensure victory—because you could well be facing multiple opponents equipped with a menagerie of exotic weaponry. These endless possibilities for equipping a spaceship mean that although the basis of the game is modeled on the classic "rock, paper, scissors" design, there's always the potential for an unexpected kind of rock to appear.

Most important of all, there's the potential for enemies to devise ingenious plans to use against you and for you to foil them in turn. The ability to communicate is just as important as the ability to wield a giant laser cannon.

Although the simplest games remain, in many ways, the most joyous, it seems to me that what gamers get from them is also simple. For more sophisticated rewards, we find ourselves demanding more sophisticated challenges. Games now have an option to become more and more complex and to utilize not only the computational power of modern gaming tech but also the communicative power of the Net. They can employ the enthusiasm of gamers to make something greater than the sum of their programming, through social gaming. When gamers combine their efforts in team gaming or their creativity in building within game worlds, they build on the foundations provided for them by the original game design. Occasionally, when games designers grasp the idea of providing new in-game tools for gamers to use, new possibilities for emergent behavior appear. This is what makes games such exciting and unpredictable things to be involved in: I log on to *EVE* knowing I can fly around and blow up spaceships, as I've been able to do in other games for over 30 years, but I also know that other things will emerge from the nebulae, other possibilities. The changes to *EVE* that Richardsson was telling me about in the bar of the Nordica Hotel lounge were to some extent putting a limit on those possibilities. That, I suspect, was the reason he was looking glum.

SERENITY STEELE

Later that night, however, Richardsson was far from glum: he was partying. Five hundred players (mostly young men, but with an incongruous contingent of girls in boots) had arrived in Reykjavik for three days of drinking, lectures, and general socializing. The gamers attended seminars on various aspects of *EVE Online* and debated things with *EVE* developers. Others played a card game derived from the video game, while still others participated in a tournament where various pilots engaged their ships against each other. Almost all of them drank beer.

One of these partygoers was an energetic young Dutchman in horn-rimmed glasses. He bustled up to our table to show off a prototype of a book of strategic maps based on the star systems in the game. He hoped that the development team might help him to bring the book to the market. I leafed through it; this was a proficient-looking tome, filled with detailed information on the *EVE* universe. The energetic man's real name, I later discovered, was Shayne Smart, but that wasn't how he was introduced to me. This was Serenity Steele, from Interstellar Starbase Syndicate (henceforth ISS), a name familiar to most *EVE* players. Steele, Smart's in-game persona, is one of the figureheads of the most aggressive and deliberate project to have emerged within a game. The ISS is a unique attempt to develop the idea of emergent behaviors based on the tools and ideas found in *EVE Online*.

Smart and his Danish gaming partner Martin Wiinholt wanted to bring a more neutral, modern infrastructure to the game world. While most of the game defaulted to feudalistic, warring tribes of players, the ISS project was designed to be something rather more capitalistic. Smart and Wiinholt intended to invent their own objectives and to bend the game to their own vision. They were not simply going to ply the markets for a quick virtual buck; nor were they going to get together a gang of ships to make friends and explode enemies. They wanted, instead, to create an alternative infrastructure. They understood that the real world was not dominated by tribes and armies; it was banks, captains of industry, and administrative organizations who had the real power. With their sci-fi alter egos already having made an in-game fortune, the pair launched a project that was "part role play, part game play" and declared themselves to be neutral to all parties. The two gamers announced their intention to add to the game world in a way that could be useful to all players, regardless of which faction they had aligned themselves with. This would be a project for everyone, not just warmongers.

The first ISS project was to build in-game space stations. Nothing strange there—plenty of other large player conglomerations had intended to build stations, too. But the ISS plan was to sell theirs as public projects. Their stations would not be private fortresses but shared, public outlets, paid for by shareholders. They would be neutral zones, forums for trade, solaces for the persecuted and the poor. The money to build these space stations (astronomical, even in a game as awash in virtual capital as *EVE*) would be raised by selling shares in the project, and shareholders would benefit from dividends paid for by the profits made by the station. To provide a sense of perspective on this, it's worth considering that the first *EVE* space station took perhaps 200 people many thousands of man-hours to prepare and was valued at around US$8,000 at the initial public offering, calculated on the basis of eBay rates for *EVE*'s virtual cash at the time.

Crucially, Smart and Wiinholt wanted to create an entity within the game that would allow players to make the most out of their time. If you wanted to contribute to a larger project or simply to have access to a neutral base in dangerous, profitable "Wild West" areas of the galaxy, then the ISS project would work for you. And in the process of making the ISS work, Smart and Wiinholt would create an unparalleled social experiment. What the game's developers couldn't create in terms of climate, cooperation, and mediation, the ISS would attempt to do. There was no way to enforce neutrality in a game of pure warfare, and that meant the ISS would have to depend on social and political maneuvering to allow their plans to work. They would have to depend on the respect of the players to let their intentions survive intact. One of the earliest tactics adopted by the syndicate was to offer shares to the local pirate groups who would most likely cause trouble, with the expectation that getting them inside the project, getting them involved, would direct their troublemaking elsewhere. Of course, their in-game finances meant that the ISS could also afford the best mercenaries to protect the project, but the investment, the project itself, would depend on gamers understanding that the ISS was a deliberate attempt to furnish a game world with new ideas and new principles.

## GAMER'S REVERIE

The initial elements of the ISS's social and political work were to be found in the business plans delivered by Smart and Wiinholt on the ISS Web site. Drawn up the way one might draw up a plan for investors in a real-world scenario, the ISS business profile outlined how the shareholder space station project would pay for itself. It told investors where the money would go and how shareholders could be expected to make a profit. The ISS masterminds' businesslike approach was to be reflected in all aspects of the overall project, with regular reports on the game's forums and far-reaching plans to rejuvenate "backwater" areas of space by building a chain of stations where none had previously existed. I was one of many gamers who bought into the project. My *EVE* friends had found themselves uprooted, thanks to wars not going our way, and soon we installed ourselves in an ISS station. We all poured money into the ISS project, and we were alternately delighted or bemused by the tiny dividends that were paid back to us by Smart and Wiinholt's online team.

A year later, this station-building project came to an end. It seems that Wiinholt and Smart could only sustain neutrality for so long, and the propensity of gamers to just want to blow things up led to wars, arguments, and, ultimately, the loss of the publicly funded stations to privately held *EVE* corporations. And so the ISS project has also moved on. Smart and Wiinholt are now attempting something even more ambitious: to drive their virtual business forward by selling off the entire ISS corporation to shareholders. This means that an organization run by hundreds of individual players will be responsible to its shareholders. The intention to sell shares in the corporation itself means that, for the first time ever, an in-game organization will be publicly owned by people other than its own players. It will be financed by the wider population of *EVE,* so that it can buy new assets, trade, manufacture, and pay back its investors accordingly. According to Smart and Wiinholt, the corporation will be motivated exclusively by the need to deliver shareholder value. The money it raises will be invested in trade and used to generate more cash by manipulating *EVE's* complex economic systems. The hundreds of gamers who play under the ISS banner will be responsible to other gamers for their virtual cash. Since *EVE's* virtual currency can be bought and sold in online markets, such as eBay, it's possible to make a valuation of the corporation: a conservative estimate puts the value of the ISS at $75,000, although it could really be as much as $150,000. And this does not include the considerable personal assets of the ISS membership.

Smart told me that the ISS idea originally developed from "a personal desire for emergent play." This is no accidental happenstance dreamed up in a gamer's reverie: it is a deliberate, grand project and will represent a lifetime achievement not just for Wiinholt and Smart but also for many of the other gamers who have sunk months of their own time into making the ISS idea into a (virtual) reality. What makes ISS so exciting for these gamers is that it says something about how they might be able to work together in games in the future. As in the case of the ISS, there's the possibility of devising your own content and delivering it to the game. There's the chance to leave a mark, to affect the game directly and change the experience for thousands of other gamers.

Games have always looked to the future, and they have also always been exercises in imagination: we can't help thinking about what else might be possible. This phenomenon seems to me to be peculiarly pronounced within the medium of electronic games. We don't tend to imagine possibilities for future books with such clarity or to imagine "What if . . . ?" when we watch a good movie. But games instill gamers with a particular desire for and vision of future experiences. They see one game and instinctively extend it into other, imagined experiences. All gamers have discovered something they didn't expect in a game and wondered what it would be like if other games offered the same kinds of possibility. The ISS project asked "What if . . . ?" for the entire future of online worlds.

Smart and Wiinholt imagined what was possible within *EVE* and then gained the confidence and trust of other gamers necessary to make it so. They persuaded many players to respect their ambitions and to sign on to the project. They encouraged people to part with vast amounts of virtual money that they had spent months of game time accruing. The ISS idea was far more than a bit of acting and playing: it was a wealth of in-game content, complete with personal quests, bitter feuds, and profound commitments. Additionally, it was something that only the players themselves were capable of in the context of that particular game. The developers would not have had the manpower to organize it, even if they had thought of it. The players who understood what the ISS project was and how it worked now look at other games and wonder when that kind of potential is going to be available to them again. In that way, *EVE* provides a model for the possible future of games.

The role of user-generated content in online gaming is becoming increasingly significant. Sure, *EVE* might be a hard-core, relatively nerdy space game, but it also delivers examples of systems that can be imitated by other games: resources, economics, communications. These are tools that allow players to set themselves goals way beyond high scores and bragging rights. Smart and Wiinholt might have been guided by *EVE*'s sci-fi premises and at once hindered and aided by the warring players, but what's most important is the emergent potential they detected in the game that inspired them. A couple of gamers used their organizational and imaginative skills to make the most of an opportunity to create something far above and beyond the service they had signed up to for 15 bucks a month.

## UNUSUAL AGENDAS

Let's take a step back for a moment and examine the significance of what Smart and Wiinholt have been up to in a little more detail. Consider for a moment that only certain elements of the expansive worlds that games offer are actually working parts of the games. Wandering through *World of Warcraft*, you know to talk to the person with the yellow exclamation mark overhead, even though the world seems to be alive with flora, fauna, and wandering elves. No matter how complex a game seems to be, it still follows certain rules. In *EVE*, you know that the space stations and spacecraft are there to be interacted with, while the stars and planets are not. The market defines how well your business ideas will work, while the modules you equip a ship with will define its abilities and limitations. This is not a complete and limitless galaxy, it is a game. *EVE* remains tightly bound to its aim of creating tales of space combat and economics. This isn't total freedom: there are strict parameters and obvious limitations. The game's creators might aim to create tools for players to go off and make their own fun, but the kind of tools they provide will end up defining what that fun is. The ISS project benefited from the open-ended nature of the *EVE* world, where players are able to build infrastructure and then exploit resources. But the players did not create that framework; they simply innovated within it. Smart and Wiinholt defined their goals based on how money could be transferred and how the construction of space stations had been implemented. This, in turn, defined the goals they were to create for other players, all in the context of a sci-fi space war. Ultimately, *EVE*'s space war genetics mean that it still adheres to some old-fashioned ideas about how games should function: players create "kill boards" to list who they've defeated, while total skill points and measures of wealth provide traditional aspirational targets for gamers to aim for. *EVE*'s emergent projects are clever, unforeseen, and often complex, but they also come laden with video game baggage.

Other games provide even more room for players to build, and they discard much of what has traditionally characterized the experience of game playing. These are games in which the process of creating things and toying with the game world is more important than achieving a high score or completing a quest. In fact, in some cases, all such targets have been rejected to create something that has no goals attached. These are less like games than like toys or, perhaps, tool kits.

These systems are occasionally referred to as "sandbox games." *EVE* has some elements of a sandbox, but goals and quests are still quite carefully delineated for the players. Similarly sandboxlike are the *Grand Theft Auto* games, which allow you to pursue vehicular mayhem for it's own sake, going crazy in the city without any reference to the missions that the game has on offer. For an example of something even more open-ended, it's worth taking a look at the absurd *Garry's Mod*, which is a sandbox experience where players are able to build Rube Goldberg contraptions, robots, and roller coasters from a wealth of tools and physics options that have been bolted on to the original game of *Half-Life 2*. There are few constraints, and there is no game as such. *Garry's Mod* is a wild, demented playground, often hosted online in the same way that *Quake* servers are, so that people can jump in and build a jet-propelled bed or a catapult for launching zombies. Players aren't logging on to *Garry's Mod* servers to play rounds of capture the flag or to work on their combat skills; instead, they log on to invent inertia tricks that lob trucks through the sky or to build spinning silos covered in gelatinous whips.

The most famous sandbox game of all is called *Second Life*. It is an online 3-D world in which gamers can create all kinds of functional objects—from houses to bicycles, jet packs to robot suits—using the tools provided for them. Like *EVE*, it is a single world, which people can log into and move around in at will. There are few constraints, which has led to numerous problems: players are quick to create weird 3-D pornography or to crash a server by generating an infinite number of polygonal penises. Give gamers an inch of rope . . . But thanks to *Second Life* jettisoning much of its gaming heritage, it has become something more like a communal operating system than a game. It's a 3-D building system, like a CAD engine, in which people chat, trade, socialize, and pursue various unusual agendas. Building, shopping, and socializing are ends in themselves for the citizens of *Second Life*. The world's users are asked to come up with their own functions for the system it provides, and there is nothing to play, although people can and do make their own games to play within the world. Much has been made of the significance of *Second Life*'s open-ended freedoms. There have even been some excellent books written about how to run an in-game business or what the economics of *Second Life* mean for real economies. In fact, the commentary on *Second Life* is so dense, so hyperbolic, that it's easy to lose sight of the significance of other games in the lives of gamers.

Anyone who has been reading through mainstream games coverage during the past couple of years might very well be surprised to learn that there are any important online games besides *Second Life* and *World of Warcraft*. In many cases, writers have found something interesting to write about—say, the socioeconomic ramifications of *Second Life*—but they have also, in my opinion, ended up delivering a skewed image of what the real significance of the *Second Life* project is. I use it, for example, as a meeting room or, sometimes, as a kind of safari. Wandering through a landscape of unfinished projects and cyberpunk lounges can be an enchanting, if occasionally intimidating, experience. If you haven't already, you should take a look for yourself. If you have an Internet-enabled PC, go to secondlife.com. It's completely free (at the time of writing) to sign up and explore.

As fascinating as *Second Life* has been to watch and explore and despite the hype, I do not believe that it is making gamers in the way that the past couple of decades of video games has done. *Second Life* is certainly an interesting 3-D Web application, but the experiences it contains are necessarily equatable with the experience of playing more traditional games. The effect it has, therefore, is quite different. Furthermore, and most important for the purposes of the present analysis, I do not believe gamers are the people who are influencing the application's future direction. *Second Life* has emerged from events and developments within gaming technology, but it represents the extreme end of a trend toward sandbox games. This trend poses some tough questions about how best to describe what these things are, what they do, and what they are for. If the connotations of the word *games* are in some way misleading, as some people have argued, then what sort of territory are we wandering into here? And what of the halfway houses like *EVE,* where so much is possible and where the ideals of gaming also remain so rigidly defined?

## USE MODELS

Games are storytelling, cinema, music, and technology, but they are also part person. They work only when we are working with them, and they require the active participation of a gamer to accomplish anything at all. *SimCity* inventor and prognosticator Will Wright observed that unless you actually play games, it's hard to judge what is happening to a gamer: "Watching someone play a game is a different experience than actually holding the controller and playing it yourself. Vastly different. Imagine that all you knew about movies was gleaned through observing the audience in a theatre—but that you had never watched a film.

You would conclude that movies induce lethargy and junk food binges. That may be true, but you're missing the big picture" (*Wired*, April 2006). To understand games, we have to be able to usefully describe how gamers themselves interact with them.

One way to describe games is to say that they are models. Thinking of video games as working models provides us with a useful perspective on how they work and what gaming is. Heather Chaplin and Aaron Ruby outline this idea in the introduction to their book *Smartbomb*, where they liken the cognitive processes required to play games to those required to understand other operational models, like orreries—the archaic devices constructed by astronomers to represent the position and motion of the heavens. "Traditional media like books and movies use descriptions (linguistic, visual, etc.) as a means of representing and communicating ideas," say the *Smartbomb* authors. "Video games use models."

The orrery of Ruby and Chaplin's example is a device used to model something real—the relative positions of celestial objects—but games aren't similarly constrained. Instead, they model things born of imagination: the 2-D adventures of a dolphin or the tale of a terrifying galactic war. Games model what it might be like to fly a hang glider, fight your way out of a military research facility overrun by aliens, or fit together falling blocks so that they might annihilate each other. They can model third-person tennis, volleyball, or bowling; or they can model the management of conflicts between armies, as seen by you, the omniscient general in the sky. Games model a tiny plumber fighting against a tide of penguins that will inevitably push him into the sea or a flying boy collecting clouds in the sky. Games model burglary and submarine combat. They model living in a house and wanting to date the girl across the street.

They model people, processes, ideas, and actions. In fact, the modeling possibilities for games are effectively infinite, since what they model is intended not to educate but to entertain. Their models don't have to be accurate to anything outside themselves, although they usually have to be coherent. The models of video games are the models of fantasies, or models designed to indulge our sensuality—streams of colors and noise where what is modeled isn't important, only how the nervous system reacts when engaging with it. Video games are a new kind of model, not intended to be tweaked and studied like the orrery or the architect's 3-D plan, but meant to be manipulated for pleasure and intellectual stimulation. War games are models of war in the same way that a kids' action figure is a model of a soldier: they might teach you nothing about soldiering, but the process—the flash of the gun and the tension of the battle— conveys enough to keep us interested and stimulated.

The idea that video games are models that require a person to complete them could also lead us to think of them as models in another sense. This alternative description was, again, best formulated by gaming polymath Will Wright, who, as well as having created some of the best-selling games of all time, has turned out to be a man with an uncanny ability to describe things in ways that have eluded other people. In June 2006, during a public conversation with the musician Brian Eno, Wright explained: "When we do these computer models, those aren't the real models; the real models are in the gamer's head. The computer game is just a compiler for that mental model in the player. We have this ability as humans to build these fairly elaborate models in our imaginations, and the process of play is the process of pushing against reality, building a model, refining a model by looking at the results of looking at interacting with things." This idea echoes what I have already said (earlier in this study) about learning to play games—that it is to some degree comparable to the scientific method. It also suggests something about how games are experienced as unfinished or incomplete. Games, as created objects, are seldom "finished" in the ways that books or paintings are finished. You read a book from beginning to end, and the words arrive in the same order, no matter your particular interpretation of the text. The same is not true of games, where the sequences of events for any given player is likely to be quite different. Even if their creators do no further programming to refine the game, it is still a working thing, a working model, with dynamic actions taking place within. As you race around *Grand Theft Auto: Vice City* in stolen vehicles, your route, your crashes, your fights with police will all be slightly different from those of any other player.

This is a vitally important point: that a game cannot function without active and continued participation from a human being. It is a model because it is also a mental model, and that mental model is never complete, is always a changing, working instance. As you play, you will think about the goals a game has set for you. In the depths of *Zelda* adventure, for example, what is important is the way you explore the possibilities of the world. The ways that the goals, story, and characters have defined your objectives and provided you with tools to meet them combine to create your experience of a game: the mental model you create for thinking about the game and solving its problems. Consciously and unconsciously, you keep the game moving by wrestling with your personal model of its goings-on. Your personal impression of the game is the model you use for dealing with it.

This, in turn, suggests something about how games are made. Through the lens of Wright's description, we can see that games are initially rudimentary models in the minds of their creators, imaginative models that go on to be turned into computer models, which are then refined and reiterated until, finally, they constitute an instance of a game that can be used to create imaginative models in the minds of a player. The mental models within players come about while playing, and this is a private experience, unique to the gamer and game.

The Internet is, however, changing this process. Games are increasingly becoming collaborative enterprises, with many people working together to achieve a range of experiences between them. (The game *A Tale in the Desert*, for example, is about the construction of a civilization in ancient Egypt. A lone *Tale in the Desert* player can achieve little and instead must collaborate with dozens of others to build temples, statues, and pyramids.) The mental models created by online games are not limited to the minds of one or two participating players but involve the minds of thousands. *EVE Online*, for example, is a vast model that is manipulated and observed by tens of thousands of people simultaneously. All these people have their own impressions of what they're interacting with, and many of them will offer their differing opinions, influencing the perceptions other players and the game developers as they do so. The model of precisely what is being played will be different from player to player, and the meaning of the experience itself is ambiguous to outsiders.

The creators of this new generation of games do not have to be satisfied with a single instance of their creation: they can now continue to develop and alter these games by releasing changes over the Internet. A patch released for an existing game could potentially change thousands of gaming experiences in an instant. *EVE Online* has gone through dozens of playable versions, each one representing a different stage of evolution of the same entity. In the case of *EVE,* which, unlike many games, has no planned "final version," the model is an ongoing collaboration between what the players want and what the creators want. It's a battle of perceptions, a contest over many rival mental models of the same game. (Here are echoes of the *Fantasy Westward Journey* incident in China, where the game world had been changed in a way that players were unhappy with, as I discussed in "A Gamers' World"). Just as we live in real communities, where the infrastructure has to be maintained so that everyone can live comfortably, so gamers' lives within *EVE* depend on collaboration with the game's creators. It has to be a model that is useful to everyone involved. Gamers have to tell the people who run the game what is wrong and what is right. The people in charge of the infrastructure are providing a service and have to cater to the needs of their customer-citizens if they want to keep making money.

If we look at all this from Wright's perspective, then *EVE* is a shared mental model in the heads of both thousands of gamers and dozens of developers, with a process of feedback moving cyclically between all those involved. The mental model is not that of one person engaging with a single model on a personal screen but a picture comprised of tens of thousands of impressions of the same model. *EVE* is not stuck in a box on an airport concourse to be occasionally admired and toyed with by a passing traveler. It is a single collaborative imaginative enterprise that exists in real time, ready to be examined and enjoyed by anyone who has Internet access and, as my friends constantly point out, anyone who has the time and patience to sink into what is a formidable and forbiddingly nerdy gaming project. Those who have had time have begun to uncover something remarkable and one of the possible future directions for gaming: entertainment that is also massive collaboration.

The ISS project is just one example of how the Internet provides us with the potential for a kind of creative democracy within games. With thousands of people investing time and money in this game, there's now a chance for a small fraction of them to take things in new directions and figure out their own projects and their own models, just as Smart and Wiinholt have done. Smart told me that he wanted to "see to what extent it is possible to influence the direction of development of a gaming universe," and the answer is very clear: it is not only possible but essential. What is perhaps less clear is whether Smart and Wiinholt are also discovering the extent to which it is possible to influence the direction of games as a whole. *EVE* represents not simply an example of intriguing game design but also an opportunity: will games grasp these ideas and develop them? They may not. It would be a disheartening dead end.

But there are other opportunities, too. The emergent behavior of gamers in online environments such as *EVE Online* represents only one way in which the relationship between games and gamers could potentially develop. The creativity of gamers could change the future of gaming in a number of other possible ways, and I look at these in "Model Living."

## Model Living

And now for a brief digression to a dreary evening in Bath, England. . . .

On celebrating someone's birthday on a freezing winter night, we adjourned our drinking to a town apartment. The place was Spartan, apart from its gaming apparatus. There was a long sofa, a large TV, and a stack of game consoles from different eras. Atop this pile there was a Nintendo Wii, complete with two wireless motion-sensitive controllers and a copy of *Wii Sports*. An evening that had already been fairly exuberant was suddenly dominated by the yelling of two 20-something women who were wildly punching the air as their supercute Mii avatars duked it out on-screen in a game of virtual boxing. The scene was bizarre but uplifting. We jeered and cheered for the flailing ladies, cracking open fresh tins of booze as we did so.

One of the people next to me on the sofa, a writer of many years' experience, said: "That, right there, is why Nintendo are the most important thing ever to happen to gaming." And I thought he was dead right. Yes, what else could matter outside a small group of friends enjoying themselves so completely? How could anything but this sudden joy in technological novelty really be important about games? How could the future of games be anything other than this kind of entertainment, on this kind of evening?

Much of what is currently written about gaming relies on just that kind of assumption: namely, that the significant future of gaming is in what happens with home consoles, in front of the family TV. I touched on this assumption in my essay about Seoul and the PC gamers of East Asia, when I pointed out how strange it seemed that their gaming culture was based around the desktop PC. Here in the West, we can't help but assume that the most important and vital aspects of gaming are going to be found in the boxes we plug into our television sets. We all have evenings of gaming like that one I had last winter, and we are all struck by the convenience and power of these pluggable entertainment gadgets. Naturally we're inclined to believe that they will be the dominant, most relevant, most important gaming platforms for the future. It is assumed that their availability and accessibility will be the defining feature of the future of gaming and that their polished games are what everyone really wants to play. It is also assumed that the most interesting events in video gaming are going to be derived from big-budget, best-selling supergames, the likes of which find their home on the PlayStation or the Xbox. For the purposes of most gaming discussion, this assumption seems reasonable enough, but over the last couple of years, I've begun to think that there are some problems with it. I've hinted at quite a few of these problems already in the present writing, but perhaps it's time to dig up a few more.

There are reasons to think that the future of gaming and of the behavior of gamers could be more various and less controlled than we might expect from the "home console" model. It might not be big companies that ultimately decide where gaming goes or how it gets there. These issues were encapsulated for me in my meeting back in London with Paul Wedgwood (described in "The Big Smoke"). At the end of our session, the goateed developer said: "The future of media isn't TV, it's YouTube. The same sort of thing seems to be true of consoles and PCs. Microsoft, Sony, and Nintendo control what you see on their screens, like broadcast television, but the PC is unconstrained. That, I think, is a very important difference." Later, listening to those words played back on my dictating machine, I realized that my interviewee was a living example of the importance of gaming and of why the difference between consoles and PCs was important. Wedgwood was a gamer who had gone pro but who needed a certain culture and certain environment to allow him to do so. And he was working with the YouTube of gaming, having entered his profession via amateur modding.

The modification of games is supported by commercial companies to differing degrees, with many of them releasing tool kits that allow direct modification of game parameters, with access to level-building tools and other custombuilt applications. Wedgwood took full use of these tools, even taking the initiative and getting in touch with the developers directly before the *Quake III* tools had been officially released. Wedgwood's team was allowed to test the tool kit, and in doing so, they seized a head start for their modification. As the project ripened, Wedgwood began to do huge amounts of promotion and marketing for his game, e-mailing news sites and promoting their work to the gaming teams across Europe. Splash Damage's mod *Q3F* was going to be one of *Quake III's* most important add-ons, and Wedgwood made sure that everyone knew about it. Once the mod had been released, Wedgwood persuaded gaming community administrators to run tournaments for the game, many of which were to be populated by the small army of *Q3F* disciples who had signed up to test the mod in its earliest beta stages.

The *Q3F* mod was a hit and, combined with Wedgwood's amiable nature, gained the attention of the original game designers, id Software. In mid-2000 the *Q3F* team were invited to visit QuakeCon, the *Quake* and *Doom* fans' official annual gathering, held in Dallas, Texas. At the convention, the team hosted their modification for their fellow gamers to play. "We manned a table and networked like crazy," said Wedgwood. "We talked to every mod developer, members of id, every hardware vendor, and just did as much as we could to promote the mod." It was the turning point for the group: the small team (then just five people) realized that they wanted to be full-time developers, not just volunteering fans. During one of the QuakeCon dinners, they pitched an idea to id's Graeme Devine (the man behind the adventure classic *7th Guest*), who told them to get back to basics and stop aiming at the sky. "He thought I was insane," said Wedgwood. "Although we had a mod, it was a straight port. We knew that we had to demonstrate a better grasp of art and technology." The team set about replacing all content derived from *Quake III* in their latest iteration of the *Q3F* mod. The new project would have a new user interface, new maps, new logos, a new soundtrack, new audio, and a complete overhaul of all incidental art materials. "In truth the community hated us," concedes Wedgwood. "We were taking this pure game that they loved, and I guess it seemed like we were just dressing it up as a portfolio piece—and there would be some truth to that idea. But we were still proud of it: we had new special effects, new models, new skyboxes. We thought we were doing something for the community." When the team returned to QuakeCon the next year, everything changed. "We had something really really polished to present," Wedgwood recalled. "And at this point we were introduced to [id Software co-owner] Kevin Cloud and to Jonathan Moses of Activision, who was the producer on *Return to Castle Wolfenstein.*"

Wedgwood's company, to be called Splash Damage after the properties of area-of-effect weapons in his favorite games, were soon going to be making commercial games. They designed the multiplayer levels of id Software's *Doom 3,* and they designed a multiplayer game based on *Return to Castle Wolfenstein,* which was eventually released freely over the Internet. As I write this, they are putting the finishing touches to a full-on commercial project, *Enemy Territory: Quake Wars,* an impressively ambitious futuristic combat game that will eventually spawn its own wave of new mods.

It was only through the possibilities opened up by modding that Wedgwood's team had been able to create this niche for themselves. Furthermore, the modding culture that has arisen around PC games has supplied the company with much of the human talent necessary to make commercial games. These were gamers who not only had enjoyed playing games but had also realized that there were ways in which these games could be improved or altered. Their compulsive reimagining of games had created something palpable. They had made new games from old, recycling and augmenting. Browsing through modding archives is like visiting a library of rewritten classics. It's as if someone were able to edit Shakespeare with pulp fiction tropes or rewrite Conrad to beef up the metaphors. There are mods that turn traditional point-and-shoot gun games into John Woo–inspired acrobatic gun juggling; others turn gung ho combat games into hide-and-seek. There are thirty breeds of zombie movie games and also the adventures of a

sentient marble. One of the most exquisite mods I've ever
had the pleasure of playing (at 4 a.m. while the sun was rising) was *Air Buccaneers*. Based on the hyperbolic sci-fi
shooter *Unreal Tournament, Air Buccaneers* is a game of archaic steampunk airships, each one floating over a smoky
gothic landscape. Players pilot the balloons and duel pre-
cariously with muzzle-loaded bombards and wildly inaccu-
rate blunderbusses. It is a strange and beautiful experience,
unlike anything else I have ever played.

This, in some way, is my answer to Chris Suellentrop's
claims about how games impinge on our imagination. These
gamers, the modders, aren't following given rules: they're
making new ones. Mods do not answer to commercial pressures or to the ideas that game developers are supposed to
have accepted. Creating a mod is a project for the inspired
and the truly committed, affording imaginative possibilities
that cannot be found elsewhere.

## HEADHUNTING

Mods have influenced some unique games and some unique
gamers. They spawned one of the most popular online
games of all time, in the form of *Counter-Strike*. That game
went on to define the European and American professional
gaming scene, from 2002 up to the present day. Mods have
also allowed many gamers to indulge their esoteric interests and their desire for expression in gaming media. One
such person is the British programmer and artist Tom
Betts, who has used modding to create some unusual art
projects. These include a psychedelic video installation
based on live modification of *Quake III* servers during play
and a manic, color-filled shoot-'em-up poetically dubbed
*Endless Fire*. For Betts, the modding scene represents a
kind of unlegislated terrain in which he could play with

bold ideas: "I realized that consoles were missing out on this vibrant element of interactivity. I could argue that consoles patronized the audience by reducing their input options and denying them access to any code or creative interface. However, this was more a case of streamlining interaction to encourage immediacy and broaden the potential audience. Its only recently that consoles have begun to reach back toward the practice of user-generated content and modification. This is perhaps not totally altruistic as console developers were seeing the benefits that modification brought to the PC game market. The mod scene serves as a mechanism to extend product life span, build communities—as well as providing a ground for free beta testing and potential headhunting."

Betts's experimental approach drew inspiration from both the games themselves and the excitement of remodeling something that had already been meticulously crafted. His approach echoes major trends in modern culture, in which sampling, cut-ups, and remixing have become essential artistic tools. Like Wedgwood's, Betts's creativity relied on the small-scale productivity that was made possible by modding culture. Without these tools, his wish to change and manipulate games would have been frustrated: "Unlike other mediums, it is difficult to translate your creative vision into a game format. The entry barriers to amateur gaming production are daunting and, when considering console platforms, almost impossible. The PC modding scene allows players to become developers without too much hassle, and in many cases, the tools the 'official' developers use themselves aren't much different. The situation becomes blurred, especially where mods provide such a high level of quality as to rival their parent software. The PC has always been a more open platform than consoles, where it's hard to comment on or alter titles without resorting to machinima techniques or advanced hardware hacks."

Betts, like many other people undertaking these small-scale, no-budget gaming projects, was thrilled by the freedoms they afforded him: "As a programmer I often code my own projects, but modding often appeals to me as a more interventionist 'punk' approach. I wanted to make artwork about games and gaming culture, so actually using the same tools and software as that culture seemed a more direct route to comment upon it. I also feel that modification allows me a route to provide alternative readings of a game and suggest other forms gaming could take. FPS games [first-person shooters, such as *Doom* and *Half-Life*] have always seemed on the verge of orgiastic screen-smearing chaos, so that is how I approached most of my mods. At the same time, I wanted the experience to be dislocated from the usual gaming environment, to draw attention to the surrounding culture of games and the issues they raise. Modding can also hold a kind of glamour due to its proximity to hacking and piracy; the idea of mangling all the menus in a game (especially the copyright screen) appealed to me. Gamers would recognize my mods from the original game and be unsettled by the direction and style of alteration, whereas nongamers were astounded when they realized the culture and software behind the work."

Where Betts enjoyed chaotic artistic freedom, other mods end up being simply continuations of projects that were started by commercial companies. Games like *Vampire: Bloodlines* or *Giants: Citizen Kabuto* were so ambitious and so enchanting that gamers fell in love with them and ended up working on them even after the respective commercial companies moved on to other things. The fans continued where normal development had ceased: fixing bugs, installing new features, and so on. One of the most impressive instances of the continuation of these "abandoned" games involves a racing game called *Grand Prix Legends*. Notoriously realistic and unforgiving, this ancient racer has long been forgotten by commercial concerns. The hard-core racing gamers who love it, however, continue to tweak and improve the ancient masterpiece to this day. The game has been enhanced in every conceivable manner over the intervening years, including a full graphical overhaul to bring it up to date with contemporary visual standards. These gamers aren't interested in the commercial cycle of new games; instead, their concern is to keep the past alive and to keep their favorite games evolving.

Wedgwood's point about consoles being analogous to broadcast media, with the major publishing companies being able to control exactly what it is that we see on our screens, was born of this kind of homegrown culture. The big console companies get to decide what games are allowed on their machines and, therefore, who makes them. They decide who can change their games and when they are to be discarded entirely. The PC, on the other hand, (so far) refuses any such guidelines. (This mildly contentious statement might end up being an untruth, because Microsoft exerts so much influence through its Windows operating system—the only viable platform for PC gaming—and that influence is increasing.)

Moreover, the Internet has given PC users relative freedom to distribute whatever gamers can make, with only occasional lawsuits to interrupt those projects that worry the copyright watchers. Crucially, broadcast systems tend to aim for one thing: the best seller, or the ratings topper. This commercial demand has warped the games market in the direction of huge budgets and mass production, a trend that has swamped the possibilities for low-scale or independent production. While independent filmmaking is still viable, independent game making has become increasingly difficult to pull off.

Digital distribution could alter this decline. Downloading games online cuts out the retailer and the publisher: gamers can buy games directly from their creators, just as they can download mods for free. Even console games developers are getting in on new ways of distributing games: Xbox Live Arcade provides an opportunity for the smaller, less popular, and potentially highly innovative independent titles to find a market. Of course, it is still controlled to some extent, and there is still the possibility that the console manufacturers will get to say what moves through their networks. In fact, increasingly Byzantine security controls on more recent iterations of Microsoft's operating system threaten the efficiency of independent production on the PC, too. We gamers just have to hope that the channels remain open and free.

Ultimately, though, it's the unconstrained production possibilities of the PC—as much a tool and development platform as it is a gaming machine—that has allowed modding to come as far as it has done. And, again, the Internet is the great enabler. The online culture of modding means that teams like Wedgwood's Splash Damage can form from people who live in a dozen different countries, in different time zones, and who can still work on the same project, to the same end. Not all modders will enter the commercial arena: and that's a good thing for gamers. For the most part, modding has been about communal gaming and personal entertainment—things done for the love of games, rather than for the love of cash. Recalling the joys of his modding days, Wedgwood told me about "development parties" he would hold at his home during those early years. His team would fly in from all across Europe for a long weekend of eating pizza and building their game. Back then, they were doing it for the fans and for themselves. The PC, Wedgwood was keen to emphasize, is still a fertile ground for such activities: gamers can be playing a game one day and rebuilding it the next.

## SUPERHERO OUTFITS

It's a month before my Reykjavik trip (described in "The Special Relationship"), and I'm in the grim northern town of Huddersfield. The view across the Yorkshire valleys is wondrous—green hills, a setting sun throwing the city below into the shade. Huddersfield itself is tired and partially abandoned. The houses are built of gray and black stone, and some have the windows boarded up. The expanding value surge led by the London property boom has not reached this far into the provinces.

I'm sitting at a kitchen table in one of those terraced Victorian houses, thinking about how the tradition of creativity in gaming goes back decades. Above all, I'm thinking about how small groups of gamers collaborate on building scenarios for pen-and-paper role-playing games like *Dungeons & Dragons*. I've joined a group of gamers who have been playing the same *Dungeons & Dragons* campaign for over a decade. The chronicle of their exploits, kept by a wry military intelligence officer from Cheltenham, has reached a quarter of a million words. Each week, they collaborate to create a story of high adventure, filled with absurd humor and ludicrously misfiring plans. Ideas are generated spontaneously in conversation, and the consequences are hilariously outlandish: heroic characters turned to mud, a fountain of kidnapped dwarves ejected from a collapsing pocket dimension, the god of travel getting lost. . . . It's their story, and no one else will ever be able to live it.

The *D&D* group is a fine example of how the promise of

creativity and of goofing off with friends makes gaming a long-term commitment—something we can sign up to and feel rewarded by for year upon year. The nondigital gaming community has long been diverse and prolific. There have long been rich, complex communities based around the "play-by-mail" games that were so popular in the 1980s and early 1990s. Then there are the war gamers and the board gamers who put everything into the creation of their miniature model worlds: the incredible precision of painted *Warhammer* armies and the authentic scenery of Napoleonic conflicts on a tabletop—sometimes taking years to create. All these impulses have found their way into computerized gaming. What these guys do on the weekends when they can meet has, in effect, been facilitated and mass-produced by the Internet. We can all get involved in gaming—hands-on, communal, and rewarding—and we don't even have to be in the same room. Games like *Neverwinter Nights* have allowed gamers to create *D&D* scenarios for anyone in the world, while the game versions of *Warhammer* games allow meticulous painting of banners and armies that can then be distributed directly across the Net for online battles.

The digital gaming world has a long and healthy prehistory of user creativity. Before the likes of *World of Warcraft* furnished online worlds with lavish graphic content, there were online games called MUDs, or "multiuser dungeons." These were text-based adventure games where Net users were able to fight monsters, talk, trade, and go on quests, all within a text-driven (generally natural language) system. MUDs were multiplayer and based entirely on what could be written into the text interface. These "worlds" were extremely flexible and allowed gamers to rebuild their content with relative ease. Like the sandbox games of today, MUDs relied on gamers to define many of their own goals and to create content. Many of these age-old text worlds are still running today, thanks to the way they directly involved the gamers in their workings and encouraged creativity.

Contemporary electronic games offer a wide array of options for personalization and content bending, and this goes a long way toward explaining their continuing popularity. *World of Warcraft*, for example, the most commercial of the online role-playing games, leaves plenty of scope for enterprising gamers to modify the game's interface, and this latitude has in turn altered and refined how the game is played. The large-scale invasions of monster-filled dungeons often depend on these third-party tweaks to the original format to be pulled off successfully. These modifications change how the information that is available to the player presents itself—with timers, notifications, and interface tweaks making the game a different experience from the vanilla game. This is how we played *Quake III* in years past: we'd tear up original configuration files to create ugly but hyperfunctional interfaces, with graphic detail removed and unnecessary prettiness expunged for the sake of efficiency. Although such alterations to the user interface may seem trivial to observers, they are crucial to hard-core players—the tiniest changes in invisible game variables were immensely important to my *Quake*-playing colleagues, especially when we were competing for league points and credibility. Like the tweaks made to racing cars, the changes made to the aspects of the game that governed frame rate and smoothness of play would decide between victory and death. The fact that Blizzard, the company behind *World of Warcraft*, didn't prohibit such modification in their game interface turned out to be to their advantage, as well as handy for hard-core gamers. Features of popular modifications have turned up in the basic interface—features that the designers hadn't thought of or hadn't been sure whether they wanted to implement.

Games don't have to be closed off, finished, or abandoned. Nor do they have to be fixed and unchanged. Learning to play might be about learning the rules of a game, but that doesn't mean that we can't aspire to change them. Of course, many of the best games are solo, solitary experiences that have been tightly scripted and carefully crafted by large teams of highly paid designers, and these cannot be modified easily. These big commercial games will also undoubtedly figure prominently in the future of games, but I nevertheless anticipate gamers finding increasingly diverse uses for messier, less product-oriented projects. The rigid masterworks that are fabricated like Hollywood films in the great production studios should only be seen as one possible way of gaming.

We will learn to value bizarre modifications and independent experiments far more than we do today: these projects are, in their own small way, the vanguard or avant-garde; and the ideas they generate may well point corporate, risk-averse projects in new directions. Just recently, a teleportation game called *Narbacular Drop* made this transition from weird private project to commercial behemoth. This clever, Escher-like game, which was freely downloadable and the result of a university project, went on to inspire the game *Portal*, a polished and humorous commercial release from Valve Software, one of the most successful games companies in the world. The evolution of *Portal* is exciting because it demonstrates how small-scale independent thinking can reinvigorate commercial game design, delivering to jaded consumers the unprecedented experience of a first-person puzzle game riddled with black humor.

But there is also more than design innovation at stake here. Games that use open-ended approaches like that of *EVE Online* can be seen as incubators for personal creativity. More than a puzzle, a blaze of action, or an intricate adventure, they offer a set of building blocks—conceptual Lego kits. Finding a project for yourself within a game world could be much like finding out what you want to do in life generally: experimentation, exploration, coping with both social and physical situations. Games are providing gamers with a lexicon in which many different kinds of creativity are possible. Gamers might want to rework an old classic or fix the bugs in a favorite game. Or, like Smart and Wiinholt, they might want to influence the direction of a virtual world in which tens of thousands of other people participate. Gamers may wish to set up a backpack manufacturing trade in *World of Warcraft* or run an online sports team. The options are open and getting more diverse all the time.

Of all the gaming platforms, the PC enables this broad approach to gaming the best, while the broadcast nature of consoles has so far found little place for these methods. In this way, the future possibilities for PC games can be seen as just another aspect of the way the Internet is now being used. Like MySpace (which provides a particular framework for music sharing and socializing), DeviantArt (which supplies a forum for showing off artwork), or even Wikipedia (in which users author and edit encyclopedia entries), games can harness our creativity by providing a medium with which gamers can develop their own esoteric projects. Games provide tools, frameworks, and inspiration. *EVE* inspired the ISS project that was devised and executed by Smart and Wiinholt (which I discussed in "The Special Relationship"). Meanwhile, on a far smaller scale, the superhero game *City of Heroes* provides gamers with the possibility for designing superhero outfits and secret lairs. Of course, these games also offer gamers limited room to maneuver, because, as in the case of a wiki (a system enabling collaborative writing on certain themes) or a MySpace page, they're designed for quite specific uses. MySpace is about being a music fan and sharing a few photos, *EVE* is about galactic conflict, and so on. These games are designed to give us goals, quests, and aspirations within a certain context. We play them because we're gamers, and our attraction to space war or goblin bashing means that we are gamers long before exposure to the medium inspires us to become modders, emergence-minded tech experts, or anything else that might develop from the act of simply playing games. Our need to be distracted, to avoid boredom, is simply the starting point. But it's a fine starting point that should not be dismissed lightly.

I would like to see a genuine divergence between the games that rely on big studios and multimillion-dollar production and the games that rely on the innate creativity of gamers. This might end up creating quite different kinds of gamers, too: those who want to sit down and be overwhelmed by *Final Fantasy*'s sweeping emotions and operatic drama and those who want to be able to tinker and mess around in their own private corners of the universe. Luis von Ahn is right about gaming having led to many "wasted cycles" of human computing (as I discuss in "Propagandists"), but perhaps the most appropriate application for the energies of gamers is in improving and expanding the games themselves. If designers can encourage gamers to collaborate with them through play, thus sparing us the hard work that modding entails, then everyone wins. We get to create content while goofing off with our friends and, at the same time, can enable gaming companies to realize even more ambitious projects.

One game that is already making moves in this direction

is Will Wright's *Spore* (aka *Sim Everything*). The game provides players with tools with which to build their own creature, a creature that has the potential to be completely
unique. Thanks to the complexity of the procedural animal
editor and the mass of options provided by Wright's team,
no two *Spore* life-forms need be the same, and this has
some pretty profound consequences for the game world.
The player evolves a rudimentary creature through various
stages of sophistication (from microbe, to animal, to sentient civilization) into what is ultimately a spacefaring culture, traveling from one star system to the next across a
vast galaxy: yet the player's experience of doing so will depend largely on the morphology of his or her creature. The
player has, in part, designed his or her own experience.

Once *Spore* players begin to explore that galaxy, they encounter other races and discover other planets. Wright's
team will not have to design the creatures that inhabit
these other planets, because the players will do it for them.
As gamers develop their own creatures, their designs are
uploaded to the Net and used to populate the universes of
other gamers. It's not a multiplayer game as such, but it
does make it possible for what someone does in one single-
player game on their home computer to have a direct (and
entertaining) effect on what happens on another computer
on the far side of the world. It's this kind of insight into
how the creativity of gamers can be harnessed that will
change how building games for gamers should be understood.

Wright came to understand this principle by looking at
how his previous game *The Sims* had inspired people to design household objects. *The Sims* is one of the best-selling
games of all time. Only a fraction of the gamers who bought
it had to produce in-game items for there to be a wealth of
extra free content. All they needed were the tools to make

their designs possible in the game world. The easier it becomes for gamers to produce in-game content—indeed, if creation of content is the game—then the more of it there will be to furnish game worlds like that of *The Sims.* This approach reduces costs for game developers, because they don't have to pay studios filled with artists. It benefits gamers, too: they are engaging with their medium creatively and productively in order to make something happen. Like Smart and Wiinholt, they will be, at least in some small way, creators themselves.

## THE PLAGUE

An interpollination of gaming ideas is taking place across our culture. Thanks to the way that gamers continually rattle around in the space provided for them, emergent situations and user-generated materials are arising in unexpected places and causing unexpected fallout. The fresh perspectives provided by harnessing the productivity of gamers have invited developers to take new paths in the development of future games. In a 2006 edition of *Receiver* magazine, David J. Edery, worldwide games portfolio planner for Xbox Live Arcade and a research affiliate of the MIT Comparative Media Studies program, described the whole phenomenon as follows: "In *Grand Theft Auto,* you can spray graffiti on the walls of the virtual cityscape. What if players were enabled to customize their graffiti in great detail? The game could automatically upload player-generated graffiti to a server, where it would be randomly downloaded by other game instances in controlled quantities. The cityscape would quickly fill up with legitimate graffiti, which would contribute to a much more authentic gameplay experience overall. And perhaps players could be enabled to somehow vote on other players' graffiti, or add to it, or overwrite it?" Suddenly the possibilities open up—the cities of *Grand Theft Auto* become the canvas of gaming artists across the world. They're not playing in the same game, like gamers do in *Second Life* or *EVE Online,* but nevertheless they're affecting each other's experiences. Games of all kinds can be transformed by the activity of gamers, if appropriate tools can be provided. We don't have to be as profoundly committed as Paul Wedgwood and his team to produce something useful or interesting—our contributions to change and content creation could be minute, but they would nevertheless count for something.

Sony's Game Developers Conference speech in 2007 focused on a game called *Little Big Planet,* which builds a traditional platform game (think *Mario* or *Sonic*) around the concept of allowing gamers ideas to construct the platform environments for themselves. *Little Big Planet*'s cute avatars jump into multiplayer games to build the game levels before playing them. These are activities that can be shared across the Internet or simply played at home with friends. It's enormously appealing both as a game and as a creative ideal for gamers generally. *Little Big Planet* presents games as malleable, communicable objects, built for gamers to customize and distort as they see fit. Things like this and like the bizarre sandbox modification of *Half-Life 2* called *Garry's Mod* are becoming facilitators of our imagination, ready to be bounced into someone else's gaming like a conceptual mind bomb: "Look at what I made." The future of games, say the big companies, is in new and accessible versions of the sandbox games: the places where gamers use games as sculptural, expressive media.

This kind of application is not limited to play. Games are also creating useful nongaming applications by virtue of their unusual approach to sharing and processing various types of information. The massively popular photo-sharing system Flickr, for example, was built using the tools developed for a failed massively multiplayer game known as *Game Neverending*. Although the game itself—a lighthearted exercise in collaborative object creation and media sharing—never made it past the beta stage, it ended up birthing one of the most important sites on the contemporary Internet. Flickr's image gallery architecture owes its existence to the gaming ambitions of its parent company—the aptly named Ludicorp—whose tools and technology concepts are used everyday in something that is definitely not a game. As the money spent on gaming increases and the things that games intended to achieve expand, so this kind of secondary application will become increasingly common.

On an even wider scale, games are leaking from one format to another. One example of this is the evolution of the *Second Life* user-made game *Tringo*. It was invented so that people would have something to play within *Second Life* and a reason to spend time and virtual cash within the user-made world. But *Tringo* soon became so popular among the inhabitants of *Second Life* that it was noticed outside the world and licensed for development as a commercial game on the Game Boy Advance. As well as being reworked and launched in the commercial format, it was polished up and then relaunched within *Second Life,* in an effort to generate even more virtual capital (capital that could then be exchanged for real U.S. dollars on the LindeX, *Second Life*'s exchange system for changing virtual to real money). *Tringo* had become a leaky object: moving between physical and virtual realities seamlessly. It was a virtual entity that had become a physical product, while still making money within a virtual world.

Other, more serious phenomena have emerged from idle play, and many of them could one day have applications beyond gaming. One of the most widely discussed examples is the *World of Warcraft* plague. This accidental virtual contagion was caused by an in-game curse called "the Corrupted Blood plague." The Corrupted Blood plague was transferred from one game character to the next and then back again, a bit like a real disease, causing massive problems for gamers as it swept through populated areas. The game's designers had intended the plague to be a temporary feature in one of the game's dungeons, but people left the area before the infection had cleared up, and so the curse spread through the game, much like a real-world epidemic.

The plague was devastating and, like real such outbreaks, was caused by the speedy, unwitting travel of gamers around their world. It was so virulent that even quarantine didn't help—servers had to be rebooted and the game code rewritten to finally curb disaster. Computers are, of course, often used to model the spread of disease, but such simulations only take into account routine behavior. What was exciting to epidemiologists about the *World of Warcraft* plague was that it was driven by the activities of thousands of real people and therefore provided a much more complex model than those generally used on epidemic-modeling programs. The random behavior and odd breaks in routine that a computer simulation is unable to predict or map emerged spontaneously from the plague-ridden gamers, meaning that they could potentially have provided a useful tool for modeling the spread of disease. This brings us back once again to von Ahn's concept of human computing, where games are about harnessing gamers and putting them to use without their even knowing. Even without having to build a new game, the models of *World of Warcraft* could potentially be of use to science as a plague-mapping tool. It might even be possible to introduce symptom-free diseases to a game and then use real people's behavior to model its spread, without their ever knowing. This, in turn, could be used to model many of the problems faced by epidemiologists in the real world, such as people with innate immunity and others who are silent carriers, not knowing that they harbor the disease. Nina Fefferman of Tufts University School of Medicine in Boston plans to do exactly that, although, at the time of this writing, she has been unable to get any games companies to perform such experiments on their customers.

Perhaps needless to say, Fefferman's ideas have not avoided vocal criticism—the *World of Warcraft* outbreak was in a virtual world, in which there is no death, and such a situation is hardly comparable to a real one. Nevertheless, the mechanical fact of it, that the gaming model could, even in theory, be used to map structures of information applicable to many different scenarios, suggests thrilling possibilities for what gamers might be able to achieve, given some lateral thinking. The games of the future might have more than one application at a given time, and many of those applications might well be invisible to the people playing them.

## THE METHOD

Back on Earth, at the *EVE* Fanfest, such metagaming applications seemed far away. Free beer tokens, smiling lab technicians from Copenhagen, polite conversation about respective socioeconomic backgrounds—it could have been the party stage of any conference in the world. Nevertheless, the kind of life and excitement that surrounds the Fanfest in Reykjavik suggests that this generation of gamers has just begun to find itself. The gamers in Reykjavik were heading out into this strange new world of emergent plans and game-driven socialization without a second thought.

They were its willing passengers, each of them paying for a ride on this journey of exploration. Gamers across the world have all bought into that in some way: games are paying for a unique kind of hi-tech progress, experimentation that would otherwise be unjustified and unimaginable.

This festival was partly a social event and partly another aspect of the collaboration that *EVE* has engendered. The massively social nature of online games makes them particularly suitable as a basis for this kind of out-of-game socializing. Gamers are able to talk over the Net and get to know each other without meeting, long before they brave an event like this. Gatherings like the *EVE* Fanfest are taking place because of the interaction of players within the game. Without this connection or conduit, thousands of friendships might never have come to be. It seems understandable, perhaps even obvious, that games would generate their own internal modes of playfulness (such as rearranging furniture in a game of *Thievery*), but the idea that they now have wider social effects remains provocative. These trends could have unique consequences: there are now millions of people interacting and socializing in online game worlds, and many of them will choose to take their relationships further—to meet at events like the Fanfest and in countless other contexts. Stories of people having met and married through online games are by now too common to mention.

Some of the people who meet outside games, like Wedgwood or like Smart and Wiinholt, see gaming as an opportunity to do something more than obtaining high scores or besting lap times. They see games as ways of networking, of making new allies and fresh work contacts. These gamers are people who are engaging with gaming productively and dragging others along with them. (*World of Warcraft* has repeatedly been called the new golf within the technology industry, because young executives are now just as likely to be able to hang out with the bosses in the Dwarven city of Ironforge as they are on the real-world golf course.)

Other gamers, meanwhile, are engaging with games in ways that have been seen as satirical, progressive, and even criminal. On the sidelines of the *EVE* Fanfest lurked one of its most notorious players, Istvaan Shogaatsu. Known to the community only by his in-game nickname, Shogaatsu has become a legendary figure. He seemed to be playing the role of legend in person, too: looking like an incidental character in *The Matrix,* he strutted across the hotel carpets in a futuristic costume and sunglasses, ultrahip piercings protruding from his handsome face. There was pointing and muttering at his presence. The *EVE* gamers knew him by reputation.

Shogaatsu's Guiding Hand Social Club is a bona fide secret organization within *EVE Online* and the polar opposite of the ISS project. Shogaatsu was the mastermind and key perpetrator behind the infiltration and massive betrayal of a major *EVE Online* corporation. It was one of the most inspiring pieces of play ever seen in a game, but also one of the cruelest and most devastating. Revealed with a flourish on the *EVE Online* forums, the attack by the Guiding Hand Social Club on the wealthy Ubiqua Seraph Corporation was a masterstroke of patience and cunning.

Initially, the Guiding Hand, who had previously set themselves up as committed assassins, had been hired to kill the CEO of Ubiqua Seraph and were to be paid handsomely for the task. Their method, though, was not the crude and difficult matter of waging war and killing the mark by martial means alone. Instead, the Guiding Hand infiltrated Ubiqua Seraph to the highest level, taking 12 months to ingratiate themselves with the corporation and gain access to its extensive resources. Like the 1930s FBI infiltrators who or-

ganized the Communist Party meetings in which suspected
conspirators were to be arrested, the Guiding Hand's own
influence on the CEO of Ubiqua Seraph arranged the time
and place of her doom. Not only did they schedule the trap,
but the executioner was to be a fellow colleague, a director
of her own corporation, and just another member of the
Guiding Hand.

When the time was right, the Guiding Hand ambushed
their quarry in space, claimed the bounty, and pillaged the
corporate coffers. A bounty that had originally seemed like
a large sum was but a fraction of what the Guiding Hand
plot would actually claim in this takedown. The mark lost
her near-priceless battleship, one of a number of limited
edition objects that the developers dropped into the game.
She also saw the assets of her corporation, which she and
her corp mates had worked for 18 months to accrue, ran-
sacked by Guiding Hand infiltrators. The Guiding Hand
members who devastated Ubiqua Seraph took some 30 billion ISK (interstellar kredits) in game money and assets, an
amount that, if taken at contemporary eBay exchange rates
for *EVE*'s virtual currency to real cash, came in at a staggering $16,500. Ubiqua Seraph was far from destroyed, but
it's impossible to gauge the psychological impact of such a
brutal strike on the players behind Ubiqua Seraph itself.
Could they ever trust other online gamers again? All of
which begs the question: are such devastating events really
smart play or just acts of outright cruelty?

This wasn't just a devious bit of gamer backstabbing; it
was a genuine betrayal of personal trust and kinship. And
it also reveals the extent to which our online identities have
new and unforeseen vulnerabilities. The excuse "Oh but it's
only a game" doesn't quite cut it when you consider that
the legitimate members of Ubiqua Seraph had poured years
of their lives into building this virtual entity. It was some-

thing they had invested countless hours into building, and the Guiding Hand actions represent a staggering act of virtual theft. Nevertheless, the action destroyed the corporation legitimately and within the parameters of the game. *EVE*'s creators quietly applauded Shogaatsu's cunning malevolence: this was emergent behavior as valid and exciting as anything that could be engineered by designers like Smart and Wiinholt. Shogaatsu had influenced a game world, stunning its population with his audacity. Whatever the ethics, Shogaatsu's work attracted many more likeminded gamers to come and see what they could achieve in the same game. This was a gamer playing the bad guy, and we could all see that he did it brilliantly.

### GRIEF CAUSED

There were other players at the Fanfest whose reputation preceded them as well. Among the most playful of these were members of the GoonSwarm, a vast in-game alliance affiliated with the online collective Something Awful. Something Awful, whose comedy-oriented review-driven Web site boasts one of the Internet's most active discussion forums, has a presence across a wide number of online games. Like many other groups who are not affiliated with a particular game, their ability to roam across many different game worlds provides them with an easy way into games communities. The 90,000 registered forum users can pretty much depend on an instant Goon fraternity in almost whatever game they're interested in. Thanks to a history of gaming exploits and the general scatologically angled humor of Something Awful, the Goons have a reputation as being a disruptive influence in many games. Their philosophy seems to be simply that people should not take anything on the Internet seriously.

In the case of *EVE Online,* the Goons started out as a mass of inexperienced players marauding around the galaxy, overwhelming their enemies by sheer force of numbers, and often dying horribly as a result of their lack of skill or experience. As the organization has grown and consolidated its assets, it has developed into one of the most significant in-game factions, though the mad verve still remains. The Goons have been derided and mocked by many groups within *EVE,* thanks to allegations of dubious tactics, but the truth is that they've largely acted within the spirit of the game. As ludicrous as their swarms of beginner ships might have been, they're a force to be reckoned with these days, and despite their characterization of *EVE* as "something awful," they work hard to maintain a lively, welcoming empire.

The Goons' most significant contribution to the *EVE* universe was a result of one of the most bitterly contested subjects in the history of the game. One enterprising gamer had discovered elements of "corruption" within CCP and publicized this fact ruthlessly and relentlessly both inside the game forums and on his own well-trafficked blog. He alleged that one of the developers had been using his administrative powers to help out the players that the developer associated with in the game world. The alliance he had helped out was the powerful and constant adversary of the Goons. This led to a continuing campaign, in which the Goons publicized more alleged corruption, including what they regarded as an active infiltration by a member of the development staff into their in-game corporations. The subject was, perhaps not unsurprisingly, an extremely contentious one for CCP. The developers denied most charges of corruption and pledged to set right the actions of their one errant staff member. Of course, being a private corporation governing a public "world," there was no reason to believe them, as the Goons were pleased to point out. Finally, just as this writing went to press, CCP made a bold move and another step toward a mature phase of collaborative multiplayer entertainment: they pledged to allow player elections that would create an "oversight committee" of player ombudsmen. These neutral representatives of the community would be allowed total access to the workings of the company and the governance of the game and, as such, would ensure that there was no culture of corruption within CCP itself. CCP CEO Hilmar Petursson told the *New York Times:* "Perception is reality, and if a substantial part of our community feels like we are biased, whether it is true or not, it is true to them. *EVE Online* is not a computer game. It is an emerging nation, and we have to address it like a nation being accused of corruption." The elections should have taken place by the time you read these words. More rhetoric? Perhaps, but even the Goons had to admit that this was a brave experiment.

Meanwhile, the Something Awful crowd has been rather more destructive in *Second Life,* where the scripting and building systems have allowed them to perform all kinds of outrageous actions. Known as W-Hats in their *Second Life* incarnation, the Goons have satirized events such as the 9/11 attacks on the World Trade Center and the assassination attempt on the last pope and have indulged in numerous other troublemaking activities. Of course, outrageousness in *Second Life* is nothing unusual, but it's the skill that many of the W-Hats have displayed that really astonishes: these are talented individuals who regularly use their remarkable talents for purely malevolent purposes. The W-Hats have engaged in numerous destructive attacks across *Second Life,* including many that have been categorized as criminal by their victims. Showers of pornographic imagery, "lag bombs" that slow a game server down to the point of uselessness—these are acts analogous to terrorism. The perpetrators of these actions are pursuing a kind of virtual anarchism, where maddening chaos is caused just because. Many of the W-Hats seem to take pride in the grief caused, and their victims have often cried out for criminal remonstration. Something Awful does not sanction any of these actions, of course, and goes out of its way to point out that people should not break the terms of service supplied by game worlds. Nevertheless, the bad seeds remain, because that's where their philosophy was rooted. These people, like those who were attracted to the ISS project, have found a tribe within a tribe—they have connected with like-minded allies. First they found gaming, then specific games, then an ethos within that game.

These anarchists, like the ISS and others, are pushing boundaries. They are living examples of why gaming doesn't force us—any more than does any other medium—to learn to obey rules. If anything, it simply gives us new rules to break, new things to subvert, and new constructs to tear down. There's always someone who wants to smash it up, always someone who will push things to the breaking point, just because it is human to do so.

All these activities seem to have ramifications for our real lives as well as our gaming ones. The U.S. State Department has been looking at how to tax game earnings since they learned that people could make money through virtual business. How long before they start legislating to protect citizens from online assault? If these actions really are criminal, as both gaming terms of service and the reactions of the victims of such attacks seem to imply, then doesn't this online anarchism have real, legal implications?

These questions raise further, fundamental questions about the future of personhood. What parts of our lives actually constitute our personal identity? Is it just the things you do, day to day, in your everyday life, or does our identity extend into game worlds? The knee-jerk reaction is that games provide us with alternate identities, masks that have no value. Perhaps that was once true, but it doesn't seem to be anymore. We're not acting or pretending: I am my spaceship, or my superhero, or my robo-suited explorer. If I have invested time and money in these extensions of my everyday life, then I deserve respect and protection.

Ideas such as these are provoking a great deal of thought among observers of digital culture. Julian Dibbell wrote two prescient books, *My Tiny Life* and *Play Money*, about the meaning, economics, and values of online life. Dibbell makes a powerful case for the contemporary social and political importance of virtual interactions, as well as summing up something about their weird, hybrid nature as both games and monetary systems: "Games attract us with their very lack of consequence," Dibbell wrote in *Wired* magazine, "whereas economies confront us with the least trivial pursuit of all, the pursuit of happiness."

## THE TRIBES

We wander into Reykjavik to take a break from the festival. Braving freezing squalls, we set out to find a famed fish bar, the Seafood Cellar. I had told my companion that this was *the* place to eat, and so we were determined to check it out. The beautiful six-foot girl on the front desk shakes her head: no booking, no food. She says she's sorry, but it doesn't seem like an apology: it seems like a dismissal. Ruefully we step back out onto the street and wander past a couple of pizza parlors. It's too cold to browse, but we didn't travel this far north to end up eating Italian. Eventually we find a bar that serves rather more traditional Scandinavian food—steamed haddock and some kind of potato salad.

It's good. Even better thanks to the music: The Smiths, the Pixies, Patti Smith, and some Elvis Costello. A young man wearing a black T-shirt and an apron delivers the food to our table. I glimpse a single metallic *Space Invader* hanging from his key ring. I want to point it out to him and offer some gaming solidarity—to say, "Brother!" But I don't. Too inane. Too far removed from my tribe. Maybe he just liked the design. I concentrate on the fish.

The talk at our table is, inevitably, about gaming. Being the more ludo-literate member of our duo, I reel off some recommendations: *Fahrenheit* (aka *Indigo Prophecy* in the United States) is, I explain, a masterpiece of modern video game storytelling. It breaks conventions, uses the medium to surprise us, and creates a worthwhile fiction. This, I suggest, is where the seemingly redundant concept of the "interactive movie" has ended up. My companion makes a note of the name, intending to buy a copy when he returns home to the United States. Then he asks, "Do you think you've played *EVE* this long because of the game or because of the people?"

Tough question. We're all familiar with the way pop culture brings dispersed communities together: we watch an episode of *Heroes* and then talk about it in the office the next day. Our knowledge of this TV show or that pop record gives us a common culture to work with. But *EVE*-like online games create something else: a cooperative project. We fight battles together; we explore the unknown together; we share jokes that are only possible within that particular game. We all have knowledge about certain games, but rather than chatting about lone experiences (as we might do when reporting on our adventures on the latest *Zelda* game), we are able to discuss group plans and group ambitions that are possible within online games. The group I play with has made this very easy. Everyone is on the same page, and we've adopted a recruitment policy of "one jump removed," meaning that anyone joining the group must know one of us from outside—whether from another online game or from everyday life. I quit playing *EVE Online* several times before I helped to assemble this group of online friends. If they hadn't made the long-term projects we have undertaken possible, *EVE* might have been just another discarded experience—a curiosity I picked up for a while but eventually discovered to be useless.

Initially, online gaming groups formed out of teams or role-playing groups (such as MUD groups). But now, it seems that they are becoming more like actual communities or tribes. Like entertainment-seeking nomads, they can move from one game to the next. If the future of games ends up being focused on user-generated works, then we will probably join projects because we like gaming with particular people we have met elsewhere. We might like the look of what they are making or how they are influencing the game world they play in, but it'll be the gamers themselves that reinforce our commitment or define how our gaming is experienced. It's happening already: the anarchic attitudes that the Something Awful affiliates have brought with their gaming exploits are just one example of how gamers are bringing real-world predispositions to gaming worlds. If my current *EVE* tribe moves to another game, I will follow because I will expect to find a similar climate of cooperation and quiet success and because I know they would only move on if the opportunities afforded by the new space are similar or better.

As elsewhere in the world of gaming, many tribes were in evidence at the *EVE* Fanfest. Subtle distinctions between what different people want from this game ended up defining who they had drinks with and what they talked about. As much as gamers can be expected to generate content and build game worlds, I suspect what they're really building in the bars of Seoul and the Hotel bars of Reykjavik are new social networks that will last way beyond the life spans of the games that currently preoccupy them.

It's telling that I recognize names from the fast-paced gung ho death-match era of *Quake III* among the most aggressive pirates and the most destruction-oriented of the *EVE* players. The manufacturers and the traders of *EVE*, meanwhile, were often architects in *Star Wars Galaxies* or obsessive *Tycoon* enthusiasts whose simulated cities were so rich in perfectly balanced futurist cityscapes as to be unimaginable by the casual player. Meanwhile, other gamers—especially those for whom mainstream games are never weird enough—seem to turn up in all kinds of unusual places, exploring the underbelly of gaming that the crowd has ignored. They lose themselves in one-man online worlds like the bizarre *A Tractor*, obsess over obscenely difficult fighting games like *Godhand*, or construct intricate military scenarios for *Operation Flashpoint*. These are people who value games as part of the sum of human experiences—as things that could not have existed before and may not exist again. They're dissatisfied with what is presented to us as the acceptable, desirable mainstream and are looking for the new and the weird. Their attitudes are not the attitudes of most gamers: they are the kind of neophiles who are interested in games because games are the newest medium they can find. Nevertheless, it's never quite new enough.

◄ HOME ►

# The Window

JUST DIRT

I've just been to California and back in around 80 hours. It was a typical games press jaunt: a few hours in an air-conditioned room, somewhere in a business district on the outskirts of a major city, a few minutes of private pixelated chaos, and hours of numbing travel.

The night I set out, Heathrow was in quiet chaos. Although the bus lane was closed, there was no sign that anything might be wrong, and only a well-informed Cockney electrician ("Oi mate, you speaka da English?") seemed to know that the buses to nearby hotels were not running. In fact, it turned out that nobody really knew what was going on, because it was too late in the evening for information. Help desks in this 24-hour airport close at 9 p.m. So I took my cues from overhearing from a lost-looking girl who was asking people where the taxi stand was. We meandered up through the multistory parking garage to the signage-free taxi area, where at least a hundred people were waiting for cabs in the rain.

You see, you can't walk and expect to get outside of

187

Heathrow. The road tunnel and runway mean that the Heathrow terminal complex is entirely cut off from perambulation. The choices are train, plane, wheels, or isolation on the terminal floor, and so I had to spend 10 pounds sterling to travel less than a third of a mile in a shared cab with the wandering girl.

I spent the night at the Park Inn hotel, which was a cross between a disco and a prison. The corporate theme was defined by rude blocks of primary color, and the elevators were filled with a gloriously kitschy rotating spectrum of light—red through blue and green, via yellow and purple—as if we were ascending to some dream of 1970s decadence. The rooms, meanwhile, were cells: bed, TV, and single steel cup and saucer, for making the tea or instant coffee. There was a deep hum from within the hotel's concrete innards.

I had an early flight. The sour-looking fat man on the passport control desk told me that I wouldn't be granted access to the United States with less than six months left on my passport. "You might want to think about that on your flight," he said, like a teacher reprimanding a naughty child. He was also unable to tell me anything more and so simply instructed me to move along. I might have been heading off to international detention, but he didn't care and seemed perfectly happy to let me into the terminal anyway.

I tried to find out more about my predicament at the information desk, which was manned by a blank-faced Scottish woman with dyed red hair. "Who brought you in?" the woman repeatedly asked, but the question made no sense. Eventually I seemed to manage to get her to understand my predicament, and she phoned someone. She shrugged, saying, "You should be fine." Then she looked suspicious and added, "Unless you know some other reason why you should not be allowed to travel?"

Worried and exasperated, I phoned everyone I know. They were, with two exceptions, asleep. No one seemed to know whether the sourpuss at the passport desk was right that I should expect to be detained or deported. I'd just have to fly to Los Angeles and find out. I boarded the plane with a sense of trepidation.

I woke up somewhere over the Rockies. The scene was spectacular: the bright blue strip of the upper Colorado River (swollen by the Hoover Dam and dotted with pleasure boats full of tourists absorbing the astonishing geography) scythed through jagged red mesas. This gave way to weird foamlike stone formations and then, beyond that, the vast earth-splitting chasms of the Grand Canyon and the mountainous monoliths of the Southwest. From 30,000 feet, it was like a divine lesson in topological extremity. With exquisite skies and an even more wonderful vista below, I was entranced.

Behind me sat an aging Californian couple, evidently not superwealthy (we were in coach class) but certainly rich in aspiration. They wore tailored shirts, Rolex watches, Chanel sunglasses. They talked quietly, and I heard the man say, "Let's see what's out there." He opened his porthole shutter. They looked out of the window at the jagged wilderness for a moment, and then the woman responded, "Mmm, just dirt." Her husband seemed to concur, and he closed the shutter tight.

We came in low over Los Angeles. *SimCity*-like zone planning was evident. Strip malls seemed to have been placed with a flick of the mouse.

U.S. passport control let me in without incident. Mentally I castigated Heathrow's sour-faced passport controller. I promised myself that I'd write a letter of complaint about how I'd been handled, but I never did.

Thanks to my frantic phone calls earlier in the day, I was

met by one of the people involved in organizing the trip. Being a lovely man, he gave me a ride to the hotel. We talked about video games. He had been a journalist before he'd decided he actually wanted to own his own house. LA sprawled endlessly in every direction. We drove past a Goodyear blimp, tethered on a disused soccer field. Roadside billboards promised "Robotic Massage" and "Grand Rug Liquidation." Later, we zoomed past the LA Galaxy stadium, where a fading David Beckham would wow the few sports fans who didn't spend their money on baseball or American football.

The video game matters that had brought me to California passed in a pleasing haze of jet lag, real-time strategy, excellent catering, and late-night typing. The modern business of games marketing is one of peculiar secrecy and lighthearted banter. My hosts were evidently terrified that I might discover something about secret projects, as yet unannounced. Following the prison theme, I had to be accompanied to the office toilet between gameplay sessions. Hushed tones in the local Starbucks conveyed a message: don't give anything away to the journalists. And, this time at least, they do not give anything away, other than the approved marketing message. The game is new, improved, and *Next Generation*. We don't bother to write this down in our spiral-bound notepads.

At dawn, I wandered around the local commercial estates—offices, hotels, blank nonresidential buildings made from glass or prefabricated concrete. There was a pleasant mist from the sprinklers that are embedded in the perfectly manicured lawns. These planes and vectors of tightly packed grass were so perfect, in fact, that they could have been rolled up and stowed away each night like a (liquidated) rug. The total anonymity of the buildings, bearing such labels as "Anetech Corp" and "Integrated Services

Inc." made the entire place seem like a facade—a video game backdrop. There were no pedestrians, just a few passing cars that stopped occasionally on the six-lane provincial boulevard. (Things aren't really bigger in the United States; they're just wider.) Patrolling these spaces while listening to Brian Eno's finest ambient work, *The Shutov Assembly*, on my cheap, verging-on-disposable MP3 player turned my early morning walk into a surrealist montage of long streets, palm trees, empty parking lots, and gong noises.

In the evening, I ate with the marketing man and a small posse of video game journalists. We were unshaven, pale, European, and out of sync with Southern California. The French editor's voice rasped like a latter-day Tom Waits record, his Parisian accent almost absurd in its weight. We exchanged anecdotes: drunken escapades on the Unreal 2 press trip, reasons to love or loathe the next batch of games on the horizon, tales of booze and electronic toys. The slow, quiet laughter and rotating storytelling seemed to suggest that we were all doing what we wanted to be doing and yet that we were all dissatisfied. Games journalists never seem to run out of things to talk about or complain about.

Slowed by jet lag and Guinness, we passed the Taco Bell building. A giant black-glass edifice in the daytime, it's an inwardly lit tower at night, betraying the late-night taco executives working hard on their charges ("We're going to design the best goddamn taco ever! We'll stay here all night if we have to!"). And so my work was complete. I traveled back to the United Kingdom relieved, exhausted. As we flew back across America, I stared out at the twilit dirt of the Rockies and thought about how many games are about terrain. I was drifting sleepward somewhere near the Great Salt Lake of Utah. I couldn't tell where the mountains ended and the sky began.

## MAGICAL CALLIGRAPHY

On returning home to Bath Spa, the partially mummified nineteenth-century town where I live in the West Country of England, I felt a sense of relief. As the train pulled into the station, I was glad to be back in familiar territory. I'm always eager to slump into familiar routines—home turf is where the slacker can take over. I forget about foreign cities and try to remember to buy groceries and cat food. I want to concentrate on the here and the now. Or I think I do.

Half an hour later, I'm rocketing through an Arabian temple racetrack in a fresh level of *Sonic and the Secret Rings*. Later I'll explore *Okami*, the water-colored adventures of a Japanese god-wolf and her magical calligraphy. Or perhaps I'll simply sit and play *Wipeout* until I'm flying down textured corridors in my sleep. I take notes: ideas for new descriptions of games and for better jokes and puns than the ones I exhausted last month. Even now, with journeys complete, I am heading off into other places.

What strikes me now, as I sit down to compose the final words of this writing, is my own ambivalence toward games and toward the culture in which I travel. I am caught between my personal interest in the games and the gamers who play them, on the one hand, and the billion-dollar business machine for which I have become a regular mouthpiece, on the other. I am troubled by the idea that games have to have some greater purpose than entertainment, and yet I am enthralled by the idea that they can be used as propaganda, art, or medicine. I want to spend all my time exploring the peculiar physics of a new game world, and yet I am compelled to write about and describe it for money.

The people who read early drafts of this manuscript detected these ambivalences, too: they thought I was confused or somewhat evasive. On the one hand, I clearly wanted to point out that people are doing more with the medium than merely entertaining each other, but on the other hand, I wanted to proclaim that the dissolution of boredom (that ennui lite that defines the early twenty-first century) is the most important achievement of gaming. Which was it going to be?

Gaming changed my life: but then don't all vocations change us? Games are a great deal of fun, but is that three-letter word really enough to encompass it all? I don't think it is. There's something else happening here, something that surfaces intermittently throughout this writing. For some people, gaming might have been a passing phase, but for the people in these pages, it's more like a life's calling: a sudden point of access to their own future. Some of us know that for however long we're going to be treading the boards of this earth, we're also going to be obsessively ex-amining, creating, and manipulating electronic games. It's our contribution to the magnificent mess of human culture.

Not that we'll think of it like that. We'll be too busy mi-cromanaging lunar bases or fighting exploding bears. As I write these words, my cargo-hauling spacecraft is undocking from a long-term base in *EVE Online*—a place as familiar to me as the street outside or the downstairs kitchen reeking of burned sausage. I'll leave the ship to make its journey un-attended while I visit some friends in *World of Warcraft* (on my "spare" PC) and make my excuses for not joining them on a trawl through the Sunken Temple. I'm just popping my head in there to check my virtual mail and to see if the auc-tion on that magic hammer is going my way. *Warcraft,* like most other online worlds, requires you to do some house-keeping if you intend to keep on top of things—doing your shopping at the auction house is just one such task. I have errands to run today, both real and imaginary.

And so, in much the same way that writers used to spend wistful hours staring out a window as they failed to compose their novels, I stare out through my screen. I can supplement old-fashioned daydreaming with an endless parade of possible worlds. Games, it seems, have no end and no distinct purpose. We have the screen to thank for this lack of precision. The proliferation of computerized screens is one of the biggest changes our world has ever seen—easily as big as the spread of the printed word or the domestication of broadcast radio. It is a conceptual shift of the kind that tends to happen without our really noticing. Television, cinema, the car, cell phones—they all changed the way we think about the world, but the revolution was slow and subtle. Now, without our consent, we find that our imaginations are at least partly defined by cinematographers and game designers—people didn't have filmic dreams before TV and cinema; they didn't have driving dreams before the car; and they certainly didn't dream of turn-based space station management from an isometric perspective, as I do on occasion. Now phones, cars, and games are ubiquitous, and screens are too. They impinge on everything from the way we sleep to the metaphors we use. Gamers dream and think gaming, bookmarks, world browsers, pause buttons, save points, and extra lives. (And that's as much a result of the Internet as of gaming—I regularly pick up books and wish I were able to hit CTRL-F to instantly summon a specific phrase, while a friend of mine regularly expresses his desire to be able to "bookmark" objects around the house, just as he can bookmark pages around the Internet. That way, he suggests, he'd avoid the daily loss of his keys.) Don't we all wish we had a "save point" before that vital conversation or that critical interview. Or maybe we just need the cheat codes.

This generation can barely imagine what that primitive

era before the screen must have been like. We depend on our windows to everywhere—television, video games, the Internet, even TV phones. Your window looks on the world with an electronic eye, and you're selectively telepathic via instant messaging and cell phones. No matter where Mom is, you can phone her up and share the news. Perhaps you can even send pictures: "Look Mom, no hands! It's Bluetooth!"

Without the screen and all the things that plug into it, I would not be anything like the person I am today. That person isn't always a fun-loving one, either. I am prone to grumble. I grumble about games and about gamers. On blogs, in magazine or newspaper articles, during barroom talk—wherever it may be, I find reasons to criticize gaming and to criticize other gamers. This grumbling is partly due to the fact that the majority of commercial games are awful, money-grabbing garbage that instill cynicism in anyone who is exposed to them for more than a few seconds, but there's a deeper reason, too: simply put, so few games are what I need them to be. Those few games, the finest fragments of the medium, are able to do what I require of them. They push the right psychological buttons and offer a satisfactory mode of escape. But most games are nothing more than a waste of time. In fact, there are so many games now that it's tough to find what we need, even if we're actively searching. There are a few accepted classics, but then there's still the problem of format and accessibility: where do you get these games, and will they work on your games machine? You can't just wander down to the library and pick up an armful of the most important games; there isn't an edition of the collected works of Shigeru Miyamoto on the bookshelf of every home. Unlike other media, there's no single route into gaming. It's a jungle, a quagmire, a mess. Over the years, many gamers have said similar things to me: games aren't quite there. There are too many inconsistencies, too many faults and problems and near misses of quality and quantity. What frustrates the grumblers is our shared suspicion that one day, with a bit of luck, games could be what we can imagine they should be. And I'm sorry retro gamers, but I think the golden age of gaming is yet to come. I have only limited nostalgia for our past.

In the last four gaming decades, there have been constant signposts, benchmarks of progress. Gamers are pushing this thing forward because, in some way, the nature of games has always inclined that way, toward the future. I've tried to contribute as a critic and commentator, championing lost or missed games or talking about what seems to have gone right with certain titles. Others, too, are working toward their own ideal: gamers build, mod, develop, play, eulogize, damage, hack, and blog games into new places, and they do it because they want difference and they want more. I think these people are dissatisfied because they are the pioneers in a gold rush: they've glimpsed the possibilities, and now they know that the riches await us, out there, somewhere over the horizon. The terrain has not been developed or refined, and there are no maps. It's proving to be a difficult journey. Perhaps this is where the ambivalence is coming from: the recognition that games mean change.

## INSTALLED *DOOM*

Marshal McLuhan, the "patron saint" of *Wired* magazine and an influential media critic, suggested that each new cultural medium changes "the ratio of the senses," or the overall balance between vision and sound, images and music. Words, which had been so important since the Gutenberg press, lost ground to cinema and television at the start of the twenty-first century, and the ratio of the senses shifted to the moving image and to the visual. As cinema came into the ascendant, its visual motifs began to dominate our imaginations and our culture. The importance of words as a medium decreased, and the importance of image, especially moving image, became central to our understanding of our world. McLuhan's ratio cannot remain static and will constantly vary over time, swinging back and forth as our media shifts and changes in its influence on us. Games represent the biggest potential change in that ratio since Gutenberg. Perhaps, even more important, our sensory ratio will now be in constant and dissatisfying flux, in keeping with the fact that games contain and exhibit all previous media, from literature to pop music, from animation to cinema. Games will not stop to find a balance between all these ingredients: change (and licensing for bad movie tie-ins) is the only constant.

I hope that gamers reach magnificent, unforeseen heights of achievement in my lifetime. I would hate to have been born a thousand years too early and miss the big bang or the wondrous future zenith of gaming. Thanks to the ambitious, visionary ideas of academics like Luis von Ahn and Nina Fefferman, I do harbor some pretty far-fetched, utopian ideas about the future of gaming. It's a future in which gamers are making games into better games simply by playing and in which games make the world a better place simply by virtue of being played. I've presented some reasons for this optimistic vision, but it nevertheless remains mostly in the realm of futurology—little better than science fiction. But perhaps that's okay. After all, sci-fi writers have managed to predict a great many of the things that have come to pass in recent years. Numerous commentators have been at pains to point out that *Second Life* was loosely defined by the concept of "the Metaverse," as conjured by Neal Stephenson's superb sci-fi novel *Snow Crash*. Stephenson defined a virtual 3-D system in which people interacted socially and economically and whose reality was only loosely based on the physics of the everyday world, rather like *Second Life:* "Like any place in Reality, the Street is subject to development. Developers can build their own small streets feeding off the main one. They can build buildings, parks, signs, as well as things that do not exist in Reality, such as vast hovering overhead light shows, special neighborhoods where the rules of three-dimensional spacetime are ignored, and free-combat zones where people can go hunt and kill each other. . . . it's just a computer graphics protocol written down on a piece of paper somewhere—none of these things is physically being built."

Retrospectively, this literary invention doesn't seem like too much of a stretch, especially given how recently Stephenson's book was written (1992), but it's no less indicative of the state of sci-fi commentary. Writers have long seen the information technologies of the future from a distance, and it has always excited them. Last year, I read a rambling collection of essays, *The Shape of Further Things,* in which sci-fi author Brian Aldiss proposed the ubiquity of mobile phones and the enormity of the Internet (or "the Big Hookup" as he called it) as he sat in his English country house in the winter of 1969. His vision thrilled me: which of today's authors are mapping the shape of things to come in the later twenty-first century? (I particularly enjoyed Aldiss's classification of science fiction as "the sub-literature of change," a label that actually only seems relevant to a very small slice of science fiction, both then and now.) Writers like Aldiss produce a great deal of material, and only fragments of it can be seen as genuinely prescient. Science fiction might have brought us cyberpunks in virtual arenas and minds sold into lifelong gaming, but these visions are still disconnected from the reality: the cheery baangs of South Korea or the heap of commercial gaming machines that lies downstairs beneath my aging TV. Science fiction glanced many of the details, but the big picture, the wide-screen fuzziness of reality, had to be written, day by day, by real people. I don't think anyone knew gaming would turn out to be quite the way it is now.

Futurologists and sci-fi writers have routinely sketched technologically advanced cultures in which leisure time (and perhaps more important, spending on leisure) is dramatically increased. They have often suspected that robots or computers would take over the mass of work and leave us idle. Did these visions, in fact, predict the leisure society of today and the problems of boredom and idleness that accompany it? Sci-fi futures often pose the problem of what to do in worlds where work has been abolished by machinery, and sci-fi characters usually go mad or end up destroying themselves in order to illustrate some allegorical point about the value of work. But perhaps the reality of it is that we just end up playing video games in the long boring gaps between our holidays on Mars. Perhaps video games have arisen because the futurologists were right and we really do risk getting bored as we're faced with ever-larger swathes of leisure time.

As I'm writing this, a link arrives via a flashing instant message box—it's a story that someone thought I might be interested in. The link takes me to a Web version of an article in *Time* magazine, first published in 1966. The article predicts the future of work in America, via an interview with the Rand Corporation analyst Herman Kahn. It reads: "By 2000, the machines will be producing so much that everyone in the U.S. will, in effect, be independently wealthy. . . . With Government benefits, even nonworking families will have, by one estimate, an annual income of

$30,000-$40,000 [$250,000 in today's money]. How to use leisure meaningfully will be a major problem, and Herman Kahn foresees a pleasure-oriented society full of 'wholesome degeneracy.'"

Wholesome degeneracy. There's another borrowed description of gaming for the list. And while we're not yet managing to live on spontaneously generated fortunes, who could deny the reality of the "pleasure-oriented society" of the early twenty-first century? The reality of poverty in all advanced nations is far from what the optimistic Herman Kahn foresaw, but he seems, nevertheless, to have been onto something. He anticipated that we would spend fortunes on creating leisure technologies for ourselves. He suspected that vast amounts of leisure time could never be unproblematic, but perhaps the real issue wasn't how idle we'd be but how far we would go in the pursuit of entertainment. No other medium is as voracious as gaming: it consumes music, comics, fiction, television, sculpture, animation, architecture, history—all in the name of entertainment.

A journalist friend of mine named Tim Edwards once sat in a bar and argued, to anyone who would listen, that games were a kind of ultimate decadence. They are as expensive to create as anything else on earth and utterly rooted in the pursuit of pleasure. These are sophisticated, arousing experiences that have few of the ugly side effects of drugs or debauchery. They are the indulgence of animal impulses without actual violence or brazen depravity. Games, said Edwards, were a trip to the gladiatorial arena without any blood spilled. This was war in exotic lands without the danger of maiming or malaria. This was a packaged, streamlined, compartmentalized orgy of the senses.

I think Edwards might be onto something, but orgiastic or otherwise, it would be ridiculous to claim that games bring only good news. Many of them, unable even to manage the bright lights and snazzy spectacle we've come to expect, only bore us. Some of us are finding games dangerously compulsive and play them to the exclusion of other, more important things in our lives. Some of us are just wasting time and money on games and game toys that were never any good in the first place. Games are not a blight on society, but they aren't a panacea either. Perhaps games, like most other human inventions, are tools—tools that we are very slowly learning to use for all kinds of new purposes. Acknowledging all those different purposes is going to be crucial to defining what it is to be a gamer.

That process is only just beginning. As of 2007, almost all of the people who have significantly influenced the medium of video games are still living and working: we're right at the beginning of this thing. The most recent entrants, the founding fathers, the whole human history of electronic games is alive now. And it refuses to falter: these fertile technologies just keep on spreading, and people keep on pushing them in new directions. In writing about games over the past 10 years, I've traveled across most of the developed world, and I don't expect my journeys in gaming to end there. My personal science fiction of gaming, the future I would like to see emerge, is not confined to the offices and TV parlors of the Western world but, instead, spreads everywhere and to everyone. If texts like this one contain a little bit of science-fiction, then it's because we want certain futures to come to pass. Just as Aldiss predicted something positive like the Internet, so I hope to predict something positive about the global gaming society to come. Perhaps, if we push hard enough, some of those predictions might prove to be more than mere fictions.

Consider this: the One Laptop per Child trade association, spawned by MIT visionaries, wants to make 100 million cheap, robust laptops and deliver them into the devel-

oping world. The overall goal is education and the allevia-
tion of poverty, but this project also places gaming technologies in the hands of people for whom games are currently an unknown, alien quantity. A new generation, a new
culture, as yet untouched by the hungry medium of gaming,
will get its first taste of our electronic frontier.

The foundation might have designed the Children's Machine, or $100 Laptop, with the intention of aiding third
world children and easing the technology gap in developing
countries, but that won't be its only consequence. These
techno-philanthropists who are conspiring to create a climate of ubiquitous, accessible, global computing could in-
advertently usher in a climate of global, ubiquitous, accessible gaming. After all, what did the foundation's software
design team do when they received their prototype laptops?
They installed *Doom*.

# The Playlist

This list is for the people who want to find out a little more about games. You can only learn so much by reading, so the list gives you an idea of what is worth playing if you want to get up to speed with contemporary games. It's hardly comprehensive, but it's nevertheless a wide-ranging survey of the interesting and the significant. Each game on this list represents a different style of gaming, and some of them are far more approachable than others. I'll try to indicate where that is so. All these games are currently available at retail or as downloads from the Internet. Of course, your best option is to find some obsessive gamers and rifle through their collections—it'll be much cheaper than buying all this for yourself. The vital tools for this expedition are a PlayStation 2 and a PC, although numerous other consoles are mentioned along the way.

## *Tetris*

The classic *Tetris* experience is on a Game Boy, but there are hundreds of variants, many of which can be downloaded for free from the Internet. *Tetris* represents the core puzzle game against which almost all others are measured. Modern alternatives and variants on the puzzle theme include *Lumines* on the Sony PSP and *Bejeweled* on the iPod. *Tetris* is almost uniformly popular and represents the kind of brain-flexing task that even the nongamers are likely to feel comfortable with.

### Robotron

Shoot-'em-ups come in many different forms, but this top-down static screen is about the purest. There are dozens of freeware versions of the classic game available on the Net. Check out *Mutant Storm* on the PC or *Geometry Wars* on the Xbox Live Arcade for a more visually sophisticated remix of the classic theme. These kinds of "manic" shooter can be overwhelming for many nongamers, but they also represent one of gaming's rawest, most stimulating experiences. Master one of these and you can truly be said to be a gamer.

### Mario & Luigi: Superstar Saga

The side-scrolling platform game has so many incarnations that an entire lifetime could be consumed in playing them. Recent classics include two released on Nintendo's portable console, the DS. Try *Mario & Luigi: Partners in Time,* which is just as good as *Superstar Saga.* To see how Sega attempted to reinvent the 2-D platform game, take a look at *Sonic the Hedgehog,* which is now available in a bundled conversion of Genesis (Mega Drive) games for the PlayStation 2. It's worth a look for understanding just how simple mechanics (run, jump) have managed to sustain such popular games for so long.

### Super Mario 64

This Nintendo 64 game remains the best instance of the traditional platform style utilizing 3-D graphics. Groundbreaking and perfectly balanced, it remains one of the greatest instances of the platform game to this day. It is also worth taking a look at *Ratchet & Clank* on the PlayStation 2 for a more updated experience, although I anticipate that *Super Mario Galaxy* will have arrived by the time you see these words, (hopefully) reinstating Nintendo as the platform game master.

## Day of the Tentacle

The adventure games, where graphical screens are navigated via a point-and-click mouse interface, represent some of the best and worst of gaming design. When they're bad, they're soul-destroying, but when they're good, they're sublime. *Day of the Tentacle*'s time-traveling plot is laugh-out-loud funny and enviably clever. The adventure game doesn't have a great many worthwhile modern incarnations, but *Indigo Prophecy (Fahrenheit)* is an interesting contemporary attempt at adventure-style storytelling.

## The Sims 2

Although imperfect in many ways, this "life sim" from Electronic Arts demonstrates some of the range that games are capable of. Events in *The Sims 2* are all about personal aspirations and social situations and demand continuous management by the player. Having a job and furnishing a house become entertaining challenges, while the sadistic will just enjoy breaking their Sims' tiny lives. For a more cartoonish, Japanese take on the life sim, try *Animal Crossing* on the Nintendo DS or GameCube.

## SingStar

*SingStar* is karaoke remixed with video games on the PlayStation 2. This is a game that makes sense in a party situation, especially if the tone-deaf people drink too much tasty punch. Worth checking out for the way the singing is rated and rewarded by the game's visual interface. Also try

*Guitar Hero* for rhythm-based rocking out on the PlayStation 2. These are two games that have made the leap from video game pastime to mainstream entertainment.

## Half-Life 2

This is the absolute pinnacle of the first-person action genre on the PC. With astounding visuals, an inspired, brilliant script, and incredibly realistic physics, *Half-Life 2* demonstrates why the first-person-perspective shooter has become one of the dominant forms of video gaming. It also demonstrates the uncanniness of a protagonist whose adventure is unwaveringly linear and whose only methods of interaction with the world involve ultraviolence and button pressing. The multiplayer is also a fun experience for entry-level online gamers. Using a "gravity gun" to pick up toilets and brutalize your enemies is peculiarly gratifying. Also see *Halo* on the Xbox for another highly accomplished first-person combat game.

## Elite

It's tough to recommend *Elite* to a contemporary audience. The classic space trading game went through many different iterations, all of which look decidedly crude today. It was the first sandbox game and brought us a balance between trade and violence that subsequent games have strained to re-create. It's nevertheless hard to see whether it would really deliver the same lessons to gamers now that it did in the 1980s and early 1990s. You can grab a playable version of this for the PC. Also in the category of PC-based space exploration, try *Freelancer* and *X³: Reunion*.

## World of Warcraft

They call it the new golf. *World of Warcraft* boasts millions of subscribers across the world, and it's easy to see why the tech-savvy Internet generation has bought into this beguilingly beautiful online fantasy. Easy to grasp and laborious to master, it's a game of wizards and warriors that supports casual dabbling and hard-core obsession. You'll need an up-to-date PC, a decent broadband connection, and a credit card to play with this oppressively compulsive virtual world.

### Operation Flashpoint

Not all games are fun. Some are terrifying. *Operation Flashpoint* is one such nightmare experience. It's a soldier sim in which death looms large. Expect to spend long periods of time lying in a ditch and praying for salvation or watching from the sky, deceased, and following one of the game's many seagulls. Intensely realistic and brutally unforgiving, *Operation Flashpoint* has created a hard-core community of virtual soldiery who drill for weeks before playing "actual" games of *Operation Flashpoint*. A more recent update can be found in the equally scary *ArmA: Armed Assault*.

### Resident Evil 4

The phrase "survival horror" was coined to describe the first episode in the *Resident Evil* series. These defining zombie games put gamers in terrifyingly unhelpful situations where mutants and the living dead mean to do harm and where there aren't enough bullets to stem the tide of the undead. Usually famed for their big frights and desperate situations, the *Resident Evil* games were updated by the fourth title, which received smash reviews thanks to its nightmarishly grim atmosphere. For an alternative and weird take on survival horror, try the PC title *S.T.A.L.K.E.R.: Shadow of Chernobyl*.

### Final Fantasy XII

The twelfth *Final Fantasy* game is a masterpiece of Japanese role-playing design. Accessible and beautiful, it is also abyssally deep, if you care to delve. The unparalleled production values and absurd, epic plot illustrate why Japanese role-playing games have remained so popular over the last twenty years. It's essentially unparalleled on other game platforms and represents an ongoing quest by Japanese development house Square Enix to create sweeping tales of a mythological magnitude.

### Oblivion

The PC's most open-ended single-player role-playing game allows players to approach the defense of their medieval realm against extradimensional demons from a dozen different angles. Ignore the peril of the world and buy a house, or simply spend your hours exploring the vast, detailed terrain. Oblivion is staggeringly beautiful and often overwhelmingly clever, with ample opportunity to accidentally become a vampire. It's just a shame about the cat people, but their ludicrousness only goes a small way to making this a flawed experience. Also to be found on the Xbox 360, it's the kind of game that should be played in schools to teach teachers what kids actually get up to these days.

### Grand Theft Auto 3

Shocking and cartoonishly violent, the *Grand Theft Auto* games are the grinning miscreant of the gaming world. Available in a number of formats, the game has become most famous on the PlayStation 2, where it caused controversy and delight in equal measure. It's a stylish game about unlikely criminality, where players steal cars, wreck them, and then steal again, on the way to the top of the tree of their virtual mob.

### WarioWare, Inc.

Instead of taking one sophisticated game idea and trying to make it last hours, *WarioWare, Inc.* gives us the minigame.

There are dozens of tiny challenges: grab a falling dollar, hit a banana, dance, dodge, shoot, skip, swim. It's a kind of distillation of possible gaming actions, each one a command, each one to be commanded. It's against the clock, quick-fire gaming and essential to not taking life too seriously.

### Civilization 4

Raise a civilization up to world dominance over the centuries. This is the scope of the *Civilization* games, encompassing all of history, from the invention of the wheel to nuclear war. You struggle to control the world, asserting the diplomatic, economic, and military muscle of your culture across the ages. It's a beautiful vision and one of the most sophisticated strategy games imaginable.

### Streetfighter 2

Like many of the games on this list, fighting games seem obscure and unapproachable to outsiders. They owe this heritage to *Streetfighter 2,* the side-scrolling, character-based combat duel that captured minds across the 1990s. The game defined how fighting games demanded that players appropriate their complicated methods for genuine mastery. It's often a hard lesson to learn, despite the initial success of random "button mashing." For a streamlined, nonbloated modern variant, try *Virtua Fighter 5* on the PlayStation 3.

### Prince of Persia

This kind of platform adventure game was most famously delivered by Lara Croft in the form of *Tomb Raider.* Nevertheless, I think *Prince of Persia: The Sands of Time* offers an altogether more satisfying experience. The best of the *Tomb Raider* games are getting old now, and the prince is doing everything Lara did, with an added (and joyous) time-rewinding function.

### Mario Kart

Nintendo's cartoon racing game is the polar opposite of simulation racing games. A world of glowing mushrooms and vibrant colors, its Super Nintendo version was the first game I truly obsessed over. It's a game that rewards skill but delights beginners. The most recent incarnation is on the handheld Nintendo DS, but I recommend the original, classic version if you can get hold of a Super Nintendo.

### Wipeout 2097

This entry reveals a bit more about my personal tastes in gaming. The "future racer" genre has always been problematic and has never quite found itself a mature instance. The best of the lot was *Wipeout 2097* on the original PlayStation, which matched ease of play with the potential to master tricky courses at mind-numbing speeds on the higher difficulty settings. *Wipeout 2097* is also interesting because it represented a major shift in marketing tactics for video game companies. Sony deliberately tied popular electronic and dance music into the release of the game, forever associating the game with the dance music culture of its era.

### Legend of Zelda: Twilight Princess

The Nintendo Wii was fortunate to launch itself onto the market with a truly great game. While the fairies-in-fantasyland theme grates with some players, it's hard to argue against the classic, open-ended delights of the *Zelda* games, of which *Twilight Princess* is arguably the finest incarnation. Transform into a wolf, ride a horse, go fishing, and save the world: this is gaming as it was always meant to be, I suspect.

### We Love Katamari

You roll a ball that picks things up: this is the principle of the katamari. It doesn't matter what the thing is; if your katamari ball is big enough, things will stick to it. And so you roll up nuts and bolts, matchboxes and cups; then cats and dogs, furniture, streetlamps, cars, houses, people; and eventually skyscrapers, mountains, coastlines, and the very sky itself. *We Love Katamari* is unflinchingly quirky, slightly irritating, and utterly charming—one of the most creative PlayStation 2 games.

### Shadow of the Colossus

This game of giant slaying has been lauded thanks to its exquisite presentation and artistic sensibility. Each of the giants is a vast, walking puzzle that must be scaled and murdered for you to be able to continue. There's something deeply sad about the deaths of the gothic leviathans, and the game's beauty is partly in delivering these mixed emotions while at the same time awing and terrifying the player. *Shadow of the Colossus* was one of the masterpieces that arrived at the end of the PlayStation 2 era.

Finally, I wrote *This Gaming Life* while playing six different games.

▶ *EVE Online* on the PC. As should be obvious from so much of the content of *This Gaming Life, EVE Online* is a long-term interest of mine. I cannot, however, recommend it to someone who has not previously dabbled in gaming. *EVE* is almost impenetrable to beginners and offers very little reward for casual play. The game can be downloaded from www.eve-online.com, but make sure your PC meets the minimum requirements to play. The game also requires that you buy time in the form of a credit card payment. Following the tutorial and getting help from other players is essential to deciphering this largely arcane and unhelpful universe.

▶ *Okami* on the PlayStation 2. Perfectly crafted and with a unique art style, *Okami* is an attempt to create a game based on feudal Japanese influences. Traditional woodcut prints on parchment, calligraphy, and old-fashioned watercolor define much of the visual style, while the story is built around Japanese polytheistic religion. The game itself is an open-ended adventure reminiscent of games like *The Legend of Zelda*. I found *Okami* to be enormously soothing— something that I don't usually expect from games.

▶ *Guitar Hero* on the PlayStation 2. A video game celebration of rocking out, this is one of the finest pieces of game design in recent memory and utterly compulsive as a result. The game requires the custom-built plastic guitar controller and a sense of humor to play. A vague sense of rhythm also helps.

▶ *Second Life* on the PC. This is like a social venue and safari through human weirdness. I'll occasionally drop by to go shopping (I bought a clockwork blunderbuss, a cannon, a new robot suit, and a selection of alien flora just last night) or visit the building projects of acquaintances to hang out and discuss games. Other times I'll just pick a direction and fly, traveling across sex shop bazaars, gaming parlors, acres of private housing, and sinister towers in the sky. Using this game for virtual tourism is a great way to frighten yourself, especially when you end up in the parlor of one of *Second Life*'s many outrageous fetishists.

▶ *S.T.A.L.K.E.R.: Shadow of Chernobyl* on the PC. It's fortunate that this horror masterpiece showed up toward the end of writing this manuscript, or there might have been dire consequences for certain deadlines. Based on a remixed version of the Chernobyl zone, Tarkovski's film *Stalker*, and the original *Roadside Picnic* novel, this is a masterwork of modern mythology. The Ukrainian development team have fictionalized the disaster on their doorstep to make something beautiful and utterly terrifying. It's a gamer's game, refusing to pull punches and demanding absolute attention. I would say it is a dream game, but it's actually more like a nightmare.

▶ *Wii Sports* on the Nintendo Wii. Watching my girlfriend use the Nintendo Wii's motion-sensitive controllers to pummel virtual opponents in *Wii Boxing* has made me better behaved than ever before. Meanwhile, I prefer some bowling and a beer.

Text design by Jillian Downey
Typesetting by Delmastype, Ann Arbor, Michigan
Text and display font: Century Schoolbook T

Morris Fuller Benton designed Century Schoolbook T for American
Type Founders in 1901. It is published by URW++.

—Courtesy www.identifont.com